**A FIDELER/GATEWAY
STORY OF AMERICA BOOK**

GREAT EXPLORERS

Joyce Grosseck

&

Elizabeth Attwood

Grand Rapids, Michigan

HISTORICAL ADVISOR

Clifton R. Fox
Department of History
Michigan State University

EDITORIAL AND DESIGN STAFF

Manuscript

Margaret Fisher Hertel
Jerry E. Jennings
Mary Mitus
Marion H. Smith

Art

Lee Brown
Ellen Osborn

Copyright 1988, Gateway Press, Inc.
Grand Rapids, Michigan

LIBRARY OF CONGRESS CATALOG CARD NUMBER: 87-081354
ISBN: 0-934291-22-5

Earlier Edition Copyright, The Fideler Company, 1981

Grateful acknowledgment is made to the following for permission to use the illustrations found in this book:

American Museum of Natural History: Page 125.

Anheuser-Busch, Inc.: Page 77 repainted by Plummer for the Fideler Company, and page 95.

Beerhorst: Pages 9 and 110 for the Fideler Company.

Bettmann Archive: Page 112.

Bibliotheque Nationale – Paris, France: Page 18.

Bristol Museum and Art Gallery – Bristol, England: Pages 36 and 37.

Brooklyn Children's Museum: Page 21 repainted by McCann for the Fideler Company.

Brown Brothers: Page 43 repainted by Stirnweis for the Fideler Company.

Burgert Brothers: Page 73.

Caffrey: Page 102 for the Fideler Company.

Camera Hawaii: Page 120.

Canadian National Railways: – Montreal, Quebec: Page 67.

The Chamber/New Orleans and the River Region: Page 107.

Chas. W. Miller & Son Studio – Manila, Philippine Islands: Page 59.

Chattanooga Convention & Visitors Bureau: Page 74.

Chicago Historical Society: Page 97.

Cole: Page 98 for the Fideler Company.

Confederate Life Collection: Page 39.

Corpus Christi, Texas, Chamber of Commerce: Page 108.

Devaney: Pages 81, 84, 131, 135, and 139.

East Africa Tourist Travel Association: Page 46.

Fairchild Aerial Surveys, Inc.: Page 83.

F. E. Compton & Co.: Page 32 repainted by Plummer for the Fideler Company.

Galloway: Pages 20, 34, and 56.

Gendreau: Page 126.

Ginn & Company: Page 58.

Great Falls, Montana, Chamber of Commerce: Page 127.

Greenwood: Page 8 for the Fideler Company.

Historical Society of Montana, Helena, Montana: Page 129.

Ike Wood: Page 103.

John Hancock Mutual Life Insurance Company: Page 128.

Lee Brown: Cover, adapted from a painting by Janet Y. Johnson.

Library of Congress: Pages 27, 30, and 66.

Mackinac Bridge Authority: Page 89.

Mac's Foto Service: Page 118.

Marquette University: Page 92.

MAS – Barcelona, Spain: Page 24.

Massie – Missouri Resources Division: Pages 122 and 133.

Matilda Metcalf: Pages 78 and 94.

McCann: Pages 23, 28, and 117 for the Fideler Company.

Monkmeyer: Page 93.

NASA: Pages 145, 148, 151, 152, 153, 154; page 149 by A. Low.

National Film Board of Canada: Pages 63, 64, 86, and 115.

National Gallery of Victoria, Melbourne, Australia: Page 113.

New York Public Library: Page 124.

Nichols: Page 48 for the Fideler Company.

North American Aviation, Inc.: Page 150.

Oslo University – Oslo, Norway: Page 10.

Paul's Photos: Page 54.

Pix, Incorporated: Page 116.

Plummer: Pages 38 and 61 for the Fideler Company.

Portuguese Embassy: Page 25 repainted by Plummer for the Fideler Company.

Radio Times Hulton Picture Library – London, England: Pages 17, 26, 31, 53, and 136.

Robert E. Peary, Courtesy of the National Geographic Society: Pages 134, 137, 138, 142, and 144; page 140 repainted by Sinkinson for the Fideler Company.

Roberts: Pages 3, 12, and 68.

Roderick: Pages 7 and 50 for the Fideler Company.

Ronald J. Wilson: Pages 88 and 90.

Saint Petersburg, Florida, Dept. of Publicity: Page 70.

Sanborn Studios: Page 99.

Scott Photographic Services: Page 75.

Sinkinson: Pages 57 and 79 for the Fideler Company.

South African Information Service – Pretoria, Union of South Africa: Page 42.

Spanish Embassy: Page 60 repainted by Sinkinson for the Fideler Company.

State of Illinois, Dept. of Conservation: Page 106.

Stirnweis: Pages 14, 19, 29, 45, 71, 105, and 123 for the Fideler Company.

Texas State Department of Highways and Public Transportation: Page 109.

U. S. Army Photo: Page 82 repainted by Lauzon for the Fideler Company.

U. S. Forest Service: Page 130.

U. S. Navy: Page 114.

CONTENTS

INTRODUCTION

"Don't sail too far out to sea. A giant sea monster might swallow your ship!" One thousand years ago, stories like this kept some sailors from going into unknown waters.

Real dangers also made it wise for early sailors to stay in familiar waters. Ships were small and made of wood. They did not have compasses* or other instruments to show where they were located. If people sailed out of sight of land, it was hard for them to tell which direction they were going. When the weather was clear, the sun, moon, and stars could be used as guides. But when it was cloudy, sailors easily lost their way.

Land travel was even more dangerous and difficult. Most people traveled by foot or on horseback. Sometimes they rode in wagons pulled by oxen or other animals. The roads they used were generally narrow, bumpy trails. In much of the world, the land was still an untamed wilderness. Fierce robbers sometimes lay in wait to attack travelers.

Since travel was so difficult and dangerous, most people stayed close to home. They knew very little about the world. For example, people in Europe did not know the continents of North and South America existed. And they had never heard about Australia or the islands of Hawaii.

Fear and ignorance did not keep everyone close to home, however. There were a few adventurous people who wanted to explore unknown territories. Some were looking for gold, silver, and other riches. Some wanted to claim new lands for their rulers and bring the Christian religion to the people who lived there. Others wanted to explore unknown lands simply for the thrill of discovery.

* Please see glossary

One by one, these daring explorers increased people's knowledge of the world. This knowledge brought great changes. Traders and settlers moved into the lands that the explorers discovered. In some places, the newcomers conquered or drove out the people who were living there. New nations were started. Among these were the United States and Canada.

Daring people are still exploring unknown regions. One of the regions now being explored is space. Like the explorers of long ago, modern astronauts are traveling where people have never been before. Their courage is helping us to learn more about our universe. With this knowledge, we can look forward to even greater changes in the years ahead.

Sailing ships long ago usually sailed along the coast within sight of land.

Leif Ericson reached North America about A.D. 1000. He and his crew of thirty-five Vikings sailed here from Greenland in search of adventure and new lands to explore.

CHAPTER ONE
THE VIKINGS
About A.D. 1000

Fierce winds drove a Viking* ship southward through the stormy waters of the Atlantic Ocean. Sometimes the small open ship with its bright-colored sail was almost hidden from sight by huge waves. A tall, fair-haired sailor gripped the tiller that steered the ship. His shoulders ached as he strained to hold the

* Please see glossary

9

Vinland was the name given by Leif Ericson to the beautiful land he found. Today, scientists believe Vinland was northern Newfoundland, where Viking ruins were found in 1961.

ship steady in the choppy seas. This man was Leif Ericson. He was the son of a brave Viking chief, Eric the Red.*

For many days and nights, Leif Ericson and his crew of thirty-five Vikings had been sailing through the rough waters of the Atlantic. They had come from the island of Greenland, which was

A Viking ship. In small open ships, the Vikings made daring voyages to distant lands.

their home. (See map on page 13.) Leif's father, Eric, had discovered Greenland nearly twenty years before and had started settlements there. As Leif was growing up, he had heard stories about other lands that lay farther west. He had decided to see these lands for himself. Now Leif and his men were sailing southward along the coast of North America. They were looking for a place where their ship could land safely.

At last the Vikings found the place they were seeking. They sailed their ship up a river and anchored in a lake. When Leif and his men had landed, they looked around them. They saw grassy meadows and tall, green trees. "How different this is from the cold, treeless coast of Greenland!" they thought.

Leif Ericson decided to spend the winter in this new land. The tall trees provided timber for building houses and fuel for keeping warm. Salmon and other fish could be caught in the river and in the ocean nearby. Later, the Vikings found thick vines bearing clusters of wild grapes. Leif named the land "Vinland," which means "wine land" in the Norse* language.

After a year, Leif and his men returned to Greenland. There they told about the good things they had found in Vinland. In the years that followed, other Vikings sailed to North America. Some of them settled in Vinland, but they were not very happy there. Sometimes they fought with the Indians who lived along the coast. Soon the colonists returned to their homes in Greenland. Far away in Europe, most people never learned about the Vikings' explorations in North America.

Today, scientists are not sure just where Vinland was located. In the past, some thought it was on Cape Cod, in what is now the state of Massachusetts. Then in 1961, ruins of a Norse settlement were found near the northern tip of the island of Newfoundland,

An iceberg near Greenland. About A.D. 982, Eric the Red* discovered Greenland and settled there.

off the mainland of Canada. These date from Viking days. Today most scientists have come to believe they were part of Leif Ericson's settlement.

The Vikings of Norway, Sweden, and Denmark are remembered in the stories and songs of Norse poets. These ancient stories tell of fierce warriors who robbed and burned towns along the western coast of Europe. Some of these warriors made their homes in the places they had conquered. Others sailed farther west. They settled in Iceland and Greenland. It was about A.D. 1000 that Leif Ericson and his men made their voyage to North America. (See map below.)

It is not strange that North America should be explored by the brave Vikings. At a time when other people were afraid to sail the unknown seas, these fearless sailors ventured far out into the Atlantic Ocean. By the sun and the stars, they guided their tiny ships across the Atlantic and discovered new lands.

Viking explorations. Some Vikings sailed westward to Iceland, Greenland, and North America.

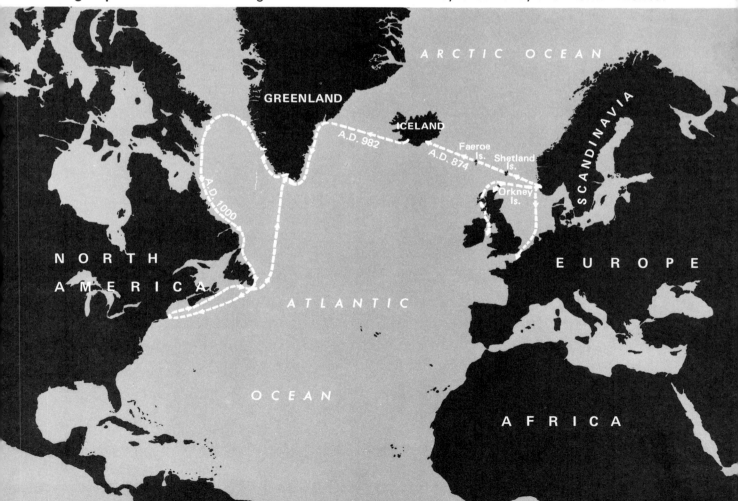

In a prison at Genoa, Marco Polo dictated the story of his adventures in Asia to a fellow prisoner.

CHAPTER TWO
MARCO POLO
1254?-?1324

One autumn day in 1298, two men were sitting in a dark prison in the city of Genoa, Italy. One of the men was telling about his thrilling adventures in the faraway lands of Asia. The other man sat at a crude wooden table, writing down this story. Suddenly, the writer looked up at the storyteller in amazement. What he

* Please see glossary.

heard seemed almost unbelievable. But his companion nodded his head sharply and said, "I have not told you half what I have seen." This man was Marco Polo, who had been captured by the soldiers of Genoa during a war. His fellow prisoner, Rusticiano, smiled at the tall adventurer and continued writing.

Day after day, Marco Polo and his companion worked in their prison cell. As the weeks passed, many people in Genoa heard about

Marco Polo's travels took him to many lands. He was away from home twenty-four years.

Marco's adventures in distant lands. They visited him so that they could listen to his thrilling stories. Within a few months, Marco Polo was so famous that he was allowed to live outside the prison. By the time the war ended, Marco Polo had completed his book.

His story, *The Book of Marco Polo*, became famous in Genoa and Venice. Soon it was copied by hand in several languages. People throughout Europe were eager to learn about the mysterious lands of Asia. About two hundred years later, Marco Polo's book was printed. Then it was read by many more people in Europe.

For hundreds of years, Marco Polo's book inspired men to search for an all-water route to the lands he described. Prince Henry of Portugal read *The Book of Marco Polo* and became convinced that it was possible to reach the East* by sailing around Africa. Later, Vasco da Gama studied it before he sailed to India.

It was a bright April morning in the year 1271 when young Marco Polo began the journey that he so vividly described in his book. With his father and uncle, the seventeen-year-old boy sailed from Venice to Acre, on the coast of Palestine.* (See map on page 15.) There they began their long journey across Asia to China. The travelers visited the colorful bazaars* of Hormuz, a city in Persia.* From Hormuz, they traveled thousands of miles farther east. Some of the time the Polos traveled on horseback. At other times they rode camels or elephants. They journeyed across plains and rugged mountains. In 1275, after being away from home nearly four years, the weary travelers reached Shangtu,* China. (See map on page 15.) Here they were welcomed by the great Emperor, Kublai Khan.

The Emperor liked Marco Polo so well that he gave him many important duties. For three years, Marco Polo was governor of Yangchow,* a busy Chinese city. The Emperor also sent him on

The Polos left Venice in 1271. Marco was only seventeen when he began his long journey to China.

many missions to distant parts of China. During his travels, Marco wrote vivid descriptions of the people he met and the places he visited. When he returned from these trips, Marco Polo told the Emperor all he had seen. Kublai Khan was pleased, for he was interested in learning more about the many peoples who lived in his vast empire.

Marco Polo served the Emperor of China for seventeen years. Finally, Marco, his father, and his uncle found an opportunity to

17

The Emperor welcomed the Polos to China. Their journey had taken nearly four years.

begin their journey home to Venice. The Khan of Persia had asked Kublai Khan to send him a Chinese princess for a bride. The Emperor chose the three Polos to escort the princess on her long journey to Persia. After the Polos reached Persia, they went on to Venice. They had been away twenty-four years.

When the Polos knocked on the door of their home in Venice, the servants refused to let them in. They thought Marco and his father and uncle had died in China. Even the neighbors did not recognize them in their rough travel clothes and strange-looking hats. Finally, the Polos went to an inn. There they thought of a plan. They invited all their friends and relatives to a great feast. Reluctantly, the servants at their home agreed that the feast could be held there. On the night of the banquet, the Polos wore costly robes and dazzling jewels. They entertained their guests

18

with stories of their adventures. After the guests had finished eating, the Polos cut open the hems of the rough clothes they had worn on their trip home. From the clothing fell sparkling diamonds, red rubies, emeralds, and pearls, which they had brought back from China.

By the end of the evening, nearly everyone at the feast believed that the travelers were truly their old friends, the Polos. Soon the news of their remarkable journey and great wealth was known in Venice and in many other cities.

The Polos brought back rubies, emeralds, diamonds, and other jewels from China.

Three years later, Marco Polo was taken prisoner during a war which Venice was fighting with Genoa. It was during the time that Marco Polo was imprisoned in Genoa that he wrote his great book.

The Great Wall* **of China.** In his book, Marco Polo described the countries he had visited in Asia.

Prince Henry of Portugal encouraged his sailors to find a sea route around Africa to the Indies.*

CHAPTER THREE
PRINCE HENRY THE NAVIGATOR
1394-1460

A light shone from the window of a tall stone tower overlooking the tiny harbor at Sagres,* Portugal. In the harbor, several ships were anchored. Their masts stood tall against the moonlit sky.

In the study room of the tower, Prince Henry was talking to a sea captain. He pointed to a large map on the table before them. "This map shows you the places along the African coast where my sailors have landed," the Prince said. "As you can see, our ships have sailed nearly two thousand miles along the western coast of Africa." Prince Henry leaned forward in his chair. "I want you to sail much farther south than any of my other sea captains," he said. "I believe that somewhere along the coast of Africa you may find a sea route to the rich lands of the Indies* that Marco Polo described in his book."

The sea captain shook his head doubtfully. "You may be right, Your Highness," he said, "but some of my men are afraid to sail so far south. No others have sailed those waters. Some think the sea there is boiling hot."

The tall Prince smiled and turned to the map. With his finger he followed the western coast of Africa. Then he said, "As you sail farther south the sun seems hotter, and the water of the sea is warmer. However, the sea does not boil. Tell your men not to be afraid. I shall reward them well if they succeed."

Prince Henry walked to the window and nodded toward the ships in the harbor below. "Take these ships and sail southward along the coast of Africa," he said to the captain. "Perhaps this time we shall find the sea route to the Indies."

Prince Henry became interested in Africa early in his life. Before he was eighteen years old, the young Prince sent ships to explore the coast of Africa. When he was twenty-one, he and his brothers led an army against the Moors* in North Africa.

By the time he was twenty-four, Prince Henry had decided to devote his life to learning more about Africa and the far-off lands of the Indies. He went to Sagres, a lonely spot at the southwestern

Prince Henry studied the sea and the positions of the stars at his observatory at Sagres.*

tip of Portugal. He built a small village high on a cliff overlooking a tiny harbor. Prince Henry worked and studied at Sagres for about forty years. He started a school and invited scholars, map makers, and geographers to come there. They studied the stars and the sea. They made maps of the coast of Africa. They trained seamen to use compasses to find in which direction their ships were sailing. They taught them to use other instruments such as the astrolabe* shown in the picture above. With the help of this instrument, sailors could find out where they were on the sea. The people of Portugal called the small village at Sagres "Prince's Town."

23

The Canary Islands. Prince Henry's sailors visited the Canary Islands, near the coast of Africa.

Later, their studious Prince became known as "Henry the Navigator."

Year after year, Prince Henry sent out ships to sail the vast Atlantic Ocean. His ships sailed farther and farther along the coast of Africa. Often his sailors stopped to explore the land along the coast. They claimed these lands for Portugal. In some places, Prince Henry's sailors built forts and traded with the people.

His sea captains met travelers and merchants who told them of their journeys through the great continent of Africa. Prince Henry was sure that his men could find a sea route around Africa if they sailed far enough.

Prince Henry died in 1460, but the Portuguese continued to search for an all-water route to India.

It was not until after Prince Henry had died, however, that Portuguese ships finally sailed around Africa and reached India. This voyage was made by a great seaman named Vasco da Gama. Prince Henry's maps and studies made possible this voyage and the voyages of many other explorers. The ships Prince Henry sent to explore the coast of Africa began the great "Age of Discovery," which continued for over two hundred years.

A map drawn in 1492. The voyages of Prince Henry's sailors began a period of great exploration.

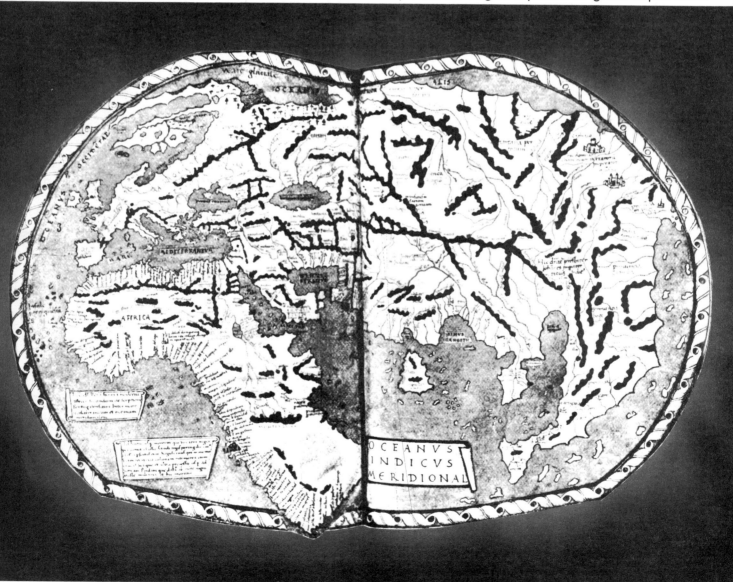

Columbus left Spain on August 3, 1492. He sailed westward to find a new route to the Indies. *

CHAPTER FOUR
CHRISTOPHER COLUMBUS
1451-1506

Three small ships sailed westward across the Atlantic Ocean. Frightened sailors shivered and grumbled as mighty waves pounded against their ships and crashed onto the decks. Some of the men were thankful that they had made their commander promise to turn back the next day.

The "Santa Maria," the "Niña," and the "Pinta" carried Columbus and his men across the Atlantic.

Tall, white-haired Christopher Columbus stood calmly and quietly on the deck of the largest ship. He was looking so intently into the night that he hardly seemed to notice his grumbling sailors. No maps could show him what lay ahead. However, he felt certain that he would find what he was seeking. Columbus heard the high, clear voice of the ship's boy calling out the time. It was two o'clock in the morning, October 12, 1492.

Suddenly a sailor shouted, "Land! Land!" For a moment, everyone was silent. Could it be true? Soon all the men on the ships

28

could see a white, sandy beach gleaming in the moonlight. A mighty cheer rose from the sailors. "Thanks be to God," said Columbus. "I have found the westward route to the Indies."*

As the sun rose that morning, the three ships sailed toward a beautiful, green island. Columbus ordered his men to anchor the ships in a sheltered harbor. Then he went ashore with some of his men, proudly carrying the royal flag of Spain. On the beach, the sailors met friendly, brown-skinned people. The Spaniards had never seen people like these. Since Columbus thought he was near India, he called them "Indians." As the Indians watched in amazement, the sailors knelt and thanked God for bringing them safely

Columbus first saw the New World on October 12, 1492. He believed that he had reached the Indies.

to land. Columbus rose slowly, raised his sword, and claimed the land in the name of Ferdinand and Isabella of Spain. He named the small island San Salvador.

For three months Columbus sailed from island to island, searching for the great cities of the East.* He was certain that there were rich cities nearby, where he would find gold, spices, and precious jewels. Although Columbus found only a few poor villages in the wilderness, he was not discouraged. He traded with the Indians for parrots, cotton, and arrows to take back to Spain.

Columbus landed on San Salvador and claimed the island in the name of the King and Queen of Spain.

Ferdinand and Isabella of Spain listened eagerly as Columbus told them about his voyage.

Then he built a fort on Haiti* and left some of his men there to search for gold. Finally, on January 4, 1493, Columbus sailed for home.

After he reached Spain, Christopher Columbus rode on horseback to the city of Barcelona. Cheering friends met the handsome explorer, who had been gone for more than seven months. As Columbus entered the royal court, even the King and Queen rose to welcome him. Then they listened with excitement as Columbus told them what he had seen on his long voyage. The King and Queen were pleased with Columbus and gave him the title "Admiral of the Ocean Sea."

No one knows when Christopher Columbus first dreamed of reaching the rich lands of the East by sailing westward. When he

Young Christopher Columbus lived in the port city of Genoa, Italy. Later he became a sailor.

was a boy, he lived in the port city of Genoa, Italy. He spent many hours at the busy harbor, watching the ships come and go. When Christopher was about twenty years old, he became a sailor. During the years that followed, he made voyages to Spain, Portugal, Ireland, and other countries.

In Portugal, Columbus heard many people talking about the Indies. The Portuguese were trying to reach these rich lands by sailing eastward, around Africa. But Columbus had a different idea. Like most educated people of that time, he believed the earth was round. He thought the Atlantic Ocean was the same ocean that lay to the east of Asia. If this proved to be true, Europeans could reach the Indies by sailing westward across the Atlantic.

Columbus spent many years trying to obtain money to make this voyage. His brother, Bartholomew, talked with the King of England

and the King of France. Columbus visited Portugal and Spain to explain his plan to the advisors of the rulers of these countries. These people agreed that the earth was round. However, some thought explorers would find a shorter route to India by sailing eastward, around Africa. "Why waste money on a voyage that has so little chance of success?" they asked their rulers. Others decided that Columbus was too greedy for money and honors. No other explorer had asked for so much. Columbus wanted a large share of the riches of any lands he might discover. He also asked to be made an admiral and the governor of these new lands.

The earth. Columbus wanted to find a water route from Europe to Asia. He did not know that North America and South America existed.

Columbus persuaded Queen Isabella of Spain to give him ships and supplies for his westward voyage.

Queen Isabella of Spain was the only ruler interested in his idea. However, she could not send out an expedition at that time, because Spain was at war with the Moors.* The Queen told Columbus that she would consider his plan when the war was over. Columbus waited for about six years. In 1492, the Moors were finally driven from Spain. Queen Isabella then gave Christopher Columbus the men and ships he needed to make his voyage.

After his first voyage, Columbus sailed westward across the Atlantic three more times. He took brave colonists to Haiti and built a town, which he named Isabella. On his third trip, he explored part of the coast of South America and some islands nearby.

During his last voyage, Columbus sailed along the coast of Central America. He was still searching for a water passage to the Indies. Near the island of Jamaica,* his ships were wrecked. Columbus and his men lived on this island for a year before they were rescued. Then Columbus returned to Spain, tired and disappointed.

Christopher Columbus died believing that the riches of the Indies lay just beyond the lands he had discovered. He was mistaken. However, his success encouraged other explorers to learn more about our world.

Columbus' first voyage. On later voyages he sailed along the coasts of Central and South America.

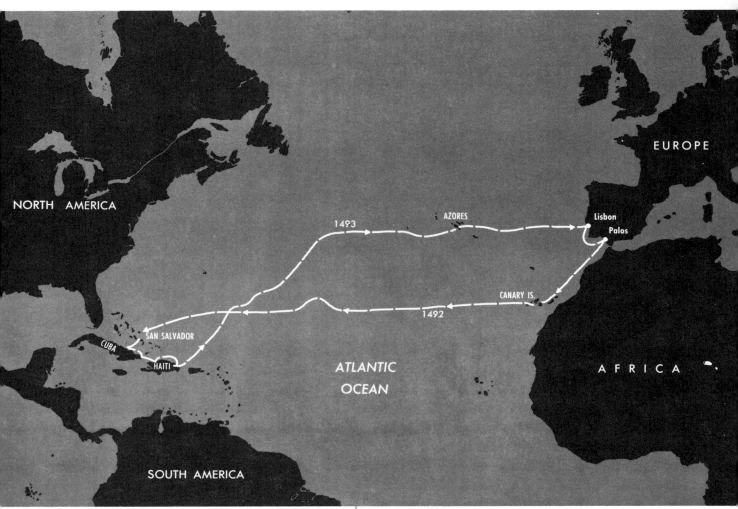

John Cabot sailed from England to find a new route to the Indies.* He reached North America instead.

CHAPTER FIVE
JOHN CABOT
1450-1498

Captain John Cabot's small ship sailed slowly out of the harbor of Bristol, England. Merchants and friends stood on the shore and waved farewell to the eighteen men aboard. "Heave to, lads!" the first mate shouted to the crew. "We'll soon be home again with gold and jewels from the Indies!"* The men cheered, and eagerly went about their duties. None of them knew that their discoveries would bring England far greater wealth and power than the riches of the Indies. Even John Cabot did not dream that he would raise England's flag on the shores of an unknown continent.

After sailing past Ireland, Captain Cabot guided his ship north-ward and then westward. He believed that this would take him to the rich cities of the Indies. Four years earlier, he had heard that Christopher Columbus had reached the Indies by sailing westward. However, Columbus had not seen the cities where spices, jewels, silks, and gold could be found. Cabot had asked King Henry VII of England if he could sail westward to the Indies and find these rich cities. The King had agreed to this plan. However, he ordered Cabot to sail far north of the route taken by Columbus. All the lands Columbus had discovered belonged to Spain.

Captain Cabot sailed westward for nearly seven weeks. One day, as Cabot stood on deck, he was startled by the loud cry of one of

John Cabot asked permission from the King of England to sail westward across the Atlantic Ocean.

Cabot's men found the sea near North America so full of fish that they could scoop them up in baskets.

his men. "Captain!" the man shouted. "The sea is swarming with fish!" Cabot and his men crowded to the ship's rail and looked down into the choppy water. Never had they seen so many fish in one place! The excited men quickly dropped nets overboard. Soon they pulled them up again, filled with hundreds of shiny fish. Some of the crew lowered baskets into the ocean and scooped up salmon, sole, and cod. Cabot did not speak as he stared across the waters of the ocean. He knew that fish often swim in shallow waters near land. "Perhaps," he thought, "we are near our goal at last."

As the sun rose on the morning of June 24, 1497, John Cabot saw a dark outline against the horizon. "Land!" he shouted. "I see land! At last we have reached the Indies!" Some of his men ran to the ship's rail. "Soon," they thought, "we will see the wondrous cities of the East."*

When they neared the coast, however, the men saw that thick, green forests covered much of the land. There were no cities, or busy ports crowded with trading ships. All was quiet and peaceful.

John Cabot ordered his crew to anchor the ship in a sheltered harbor. Then he went ashore with some of his men. They noticed that some of the trees had been cut down with crude axes. They also found snares that had been set to catch wild animals. These things proved that human beings lived nearby. However, the explorers did not catch sight of any of these people.

Cabot led his men to the top of a nearby hill. Solemnly, he raised the flag of England and watched it billow in the fresh, summer breeze. Cabot looked all around him. "I claim this land

Cabot landed along the eastern coast of North America and raised the flag of England.

in the name of King Henry VII of England," he said. Today, no one knows for sure just where Cabot and his men landed. But many historians think it was on Cape Breton Island, in what is now the Canadian province of Nova Scotia.* (See map, page 41.)

Cabot and his men sailed along the coast of North America for about three weeks. Sometimes they stopped and explored the land. Finally, there was only a little food left, and Cabot decided to return to England. Although they had seen no cities or people, he was not discouraged. "We shall find the rich cities when we can sail farther south along this coast," Cabot told his crew. Then the explorers began the long voyage home.

When John Cabot arrived in London, he had nothing to show the King except a bone needle* and some of the snares that he had found. However, the King was pleased to hear about the land Cabot had claimed for England. He rewarded him with money and promised to provide ships and men for a second voyage westward.

In 1498, John Cabot tried once again to find the rich cities of the East. This time he took five ships and a large supply of cloth, lace, and other goods. Cabot hoped to exchange these goods for spices and precious stones when he reached the great trading centers of the Indies.

Before long, a storm forced one of the ships to turn back to England. No one knows for sure what happened to Cabot and the other four ships. Some historians believe that they were lost at sea. Others think that Cabot again reached the coast of North America and then returned to England safely.

As time passed, other explorers sailed westward across the Atlantic Ocean. They finally realized that the land Cabot had reached was not part of Asia after all. Instead, it was a vast new continent. This continent became known as North America. At first, North America was only an obstacle to explorers who were searching for a western route to the Indies. Years later, however, the people of England learned the value of Cabot's discovery. English colonists came to make their homes along the eastern coast of North America. England was able to claim these lands because of John Cabot's great voyage.

Cabot's voyage to North America in 1497 gave England a claim to lands in the New World.

The city of Cape Town is on the southwest coast of Africa, close to the Cape of Good Hope.

CHAPTER SIX

VASCO DA GAMA
1469?-1524

Vasco da Gama stood on the deck of his small ship. Rain lashed his face and soaked through his clothes. It was late in November, in 1497. More than four months had passed since he had left Lisbon,* Portugal, with four small ships. He had sailed southward through the Atlantic Ocean for thousands of miles. (See map on page 49.) Terrible storms had damaged his ships, but they had sailed on. Finally, they had sailed around the Cape of Good Hope at the southern tip of Africa.

Vasco da Gama led his four small ships around the Cape of Good Hope at the southern tip of Africa.

"What lies ahead?" Da Gama wondered, as he stared into the rain and darkness. He could only guess, for no other Europeans had ever sailed this far beyond the southern tip of Africa.

Vasco da Gama was not afraid of the unknown seas. He faced a greater danger aboard his ships. His men were frightened, and talked of seizing the ships and turning back. At the thought, his eyes blazed with anger. Da Gama knew that somewhere beyond him to the east was India. He would find it, or never return to Portugal!

Now, one of the ships in the fleet sailed nearer. On the deck, Da Gama could see the ship's captain. Then he heard the captain shout, "We must turn back, or our men will kill us and sail the ships home themselves!"

Vasco da Gama was angry. "How could my bravest captain make this request?" he wondered. Then he thought, "He must be trying to warn me that this is what the men are planning to do. I must act quickly or we shall never reach India."

Soon Da Gama thought of a plan. He called his crew together. "If I agree to turn back to Portugal," he told the grumbling sailors, "you must sign a paper telling the King that you forced me to do this." Eagerly, the men agreed. Then Da Gama chose the sailors who knew how to guide the ships home. He ordered them to go to a cabin below deck. When they gathered in the cabin to sign the paper, however, the door was suddenly thrown open. There stood several of Da Gama's loyal men, armed with pistols. Quickly, they seized the sailors in the cabin and put them in chains. Then Da Gama gathered all the instruments they had used to guide the ships through the vast Atlantic Ocean. Standing before his crew, he held the instruments high over his head. Then he turned and threw them into the sea.

Da Gama threw the ships' instruments overboard to prevent his men from sailing home.

"Now," Vasco da Gama said sternly, "we shall sail with God as our pilot. If we deserve His mercy, we shall come safely to India." The fearless Vasco da Gama had left his men no choice. They could not turn back. They could only follow him onward.

For more than four months, the small fleet sailed northward along the east coast of Africa. During the voyage, the ships stopped at several places along the coast. Finally, in April of 1498, they reached the town of Malindi. (See map on page 49.) Here Da Gama and his men traded with friendly Indian merchants. The merchants provided them with a skilled Arab* seaman to guide their ships across the Indian Ocean.

From Malindi,* Vasco da Gama's ships sailed eastward across the Indian Ocean to India.

Vasco da Gama and his men sailed eastward across the Indian Ocean for over three weeks. At last they heard the lookout shout, "Land ho!" There before them lay India, shadowy and purple against the horizon. Vasco da Gama and his men knelt down on the deck and thanked God for bringing them safely to their destination. Then Da Gama rose and looked at the land before him. He, Vasco da Gama, had found the sea route to the rich lands of the East.* Eagerly, Da Gama and his men sailed on. Soon they could see wide beaches along India's southwestern shores. For a day and a night, the fleet sailed southward along the coast. At last, early on the morning of May 20, 1498, Vasco da Gama arrived at the city of Calicut, India.

When the Portuguese explorers reached the busy harbor at Calicut, they saw many ships crowding the water front. Their bright-colored sails billowed in the warm breeze. Sailors were unloading cargoes of cinnamon, cloves, ginger, and pepper from many of the other ships in the harbor. Da Gama was eager to take back some of these valuable spices to Portugal.

Vasco da Gama visited the ruler of Calicut. He told him that the King of Portugal wanted their countries to be friends and to trade with one another. He said that Portugal would send ships loaded with gold, silver, and cloth to India. In return, Portuguese ships would take back spices and precious stones. The ruler was friendly. It seemed to Da Gama that he would agree to this plan.

When the Arab merchants in Calicut heard about Da Gama's visit, however, they were angry. They did not want the ruler to allow the Portuguese to trade in Calicut. These merchants had been sending spices and jewels over slow, dangerous routes to the countries of Europe for many years. They knew that Da Gama had discovered a better, all-water route to India. They were afraid that Portugal would send many ships to take back cargoes of spices and precious stones. This would ruin their profitable business. They tried to convince the ruler that Portugal wanted to conquer India.

Although Vasco da Gama remained in Calicut for more than three months, he could not persuade the ruler to trade with Portugal. However, the ruler did agree that Da Gama could buy enough spices and jewels to fill his ships. In August, Da Gama decided to return to Portugal.

In September of 1499, after having sailed nearly 24,000 miles, Vasco da Gama arrived home. When he sailed into the harbor at Lisbon, the King of Portugal was waiting to welcome him. The King had already heard the news that Da Gama had found an

In India, Vasco da Gama visited the ruler of Calicut. He told him that Portugal wanted to trade gold, silver, and cloth for spices and jewels.

eastern route to India. He listened eagerly while Da Gama told him of the spices and jewels he had brought back with him. The King honored Vasco da Gama by making him a nobleman. Later he gave him the title "Admiral of the Indian Seas," and the right to trade in India.

Vasco da Gama's discovery of the sea route to India brought wealth and honor to himself and to his country. For the first time, Europeans could sail by an all-water route to the rich lands of the East.

Vasco da Gama's voyage made it possible for Europeans to reach the rich lands of the East* by water.

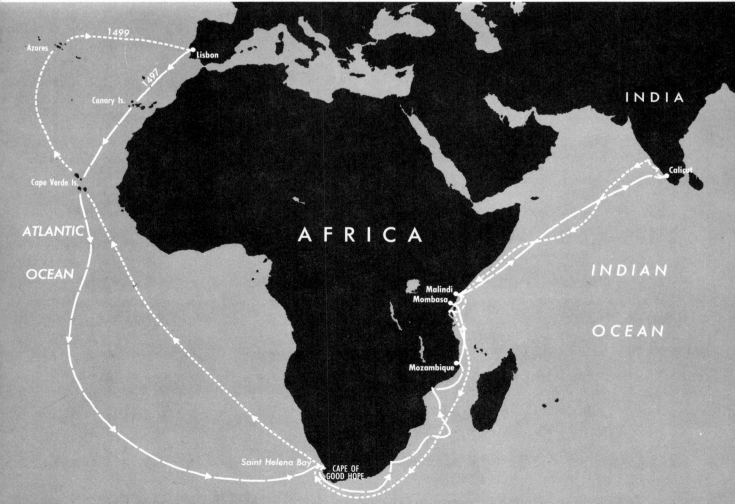

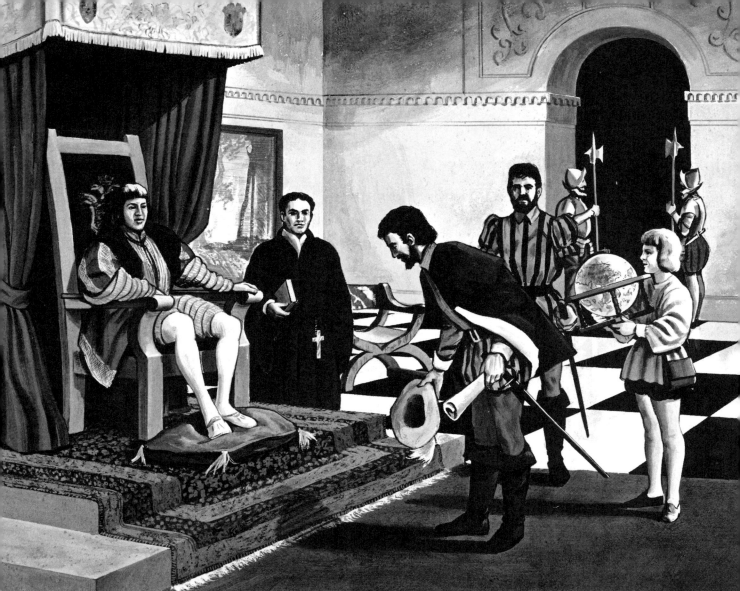

Ferdinand Magellan told the King of Spain that he could reach the Spice Islands* by sailing west.

CHAPTER SEVEN
FERDINAND MAGELLAN
1480?-1521

A Portuguese sea captain bowed before the King of Spain. "Your Majesty," he said, "I am Ferdinand Magellan." Young King Charles smiled at the rugged seaman. "I have heard of you," the King said. "Why have you come to see me?"

50

"Your Majesty," said Magellan, "when I was a soldier fighting against the Arabs* in Africa and India, I saw Portuguese ships carrying back great fortunes in silks and jewels to my country. Later, I visited the East Indies* while I was an officer in the Portuguese navy. There, I saw huge quantities of nutmeg, cloves, and other spices being loaded on sailing ships to be taken back to Portugal. The treasury of Portugal now overflows with gold from this profitable trade with the East.* I have a plan that will make it possible for Spain to share in this trade."

The young King nodded his head thoughtfully. "I would be most interested in such a plan," he said, "but Spain has a solemn treaty with Portugal. In this treaty we agreed on a boundary line that

Magellan found a westward route to Asia and proved that the world is round.

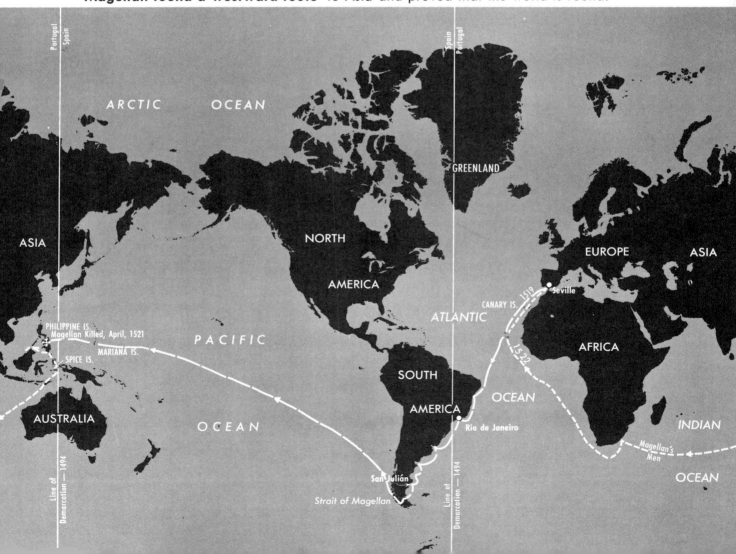

would run all the way around the world. This line divides the world into an eastern half and a western half. (See map on page 51.) Portugal may trade with lands that are in the eastern half, and Spain may trade in the west. The spices come from Portuguese territory. Spaniards do not have the right to sail there."

Magellan looked boldly at the Spanish King. "All the spices that Portuguese ships bring from the Indies come from a group of islands called the Spice Islands,"* he said. "I am convinced that these islands are on Spain's side of the boundary line and, therefore, belong to Spain."

The captain's eyes flashed as he continued, "I explored these islands myself," he said. "I made careful observations of the sun and the stars to determine their exact location. I secretly visited the royal chartroom of the palace at Lisbon* to study maps and reports made by other Portuguese sailors. I am certain that the Spice Islands belong to Spain and not to Portugal. I told this to my King, but he would not listen to me. He became so angry that he no longer wants my service or my loyalty. Now I ask your permission to sail to the Spice Islands. When I return, my ships will be filled with valuable spices for Spain."

King Charles frowned thoughtfully. "How will you reach the Spice Islands?" he asked. "You cannot sail around Africa. The route which Vasco da Gama discovered is carefully guarded by the Portuguese. (See map on page 49.) Portugal now controls much of the coasts of Africa and India. Its powerful navy would capture Spanish ships that sailed those waters."

Ferdinand Magellan held up a large, leather globe on which were painted the lands and seas of the world that were known at that time. He pointed to the vast continent of South America. "Your Majesty," said Magellan, "I plan to sail westward across

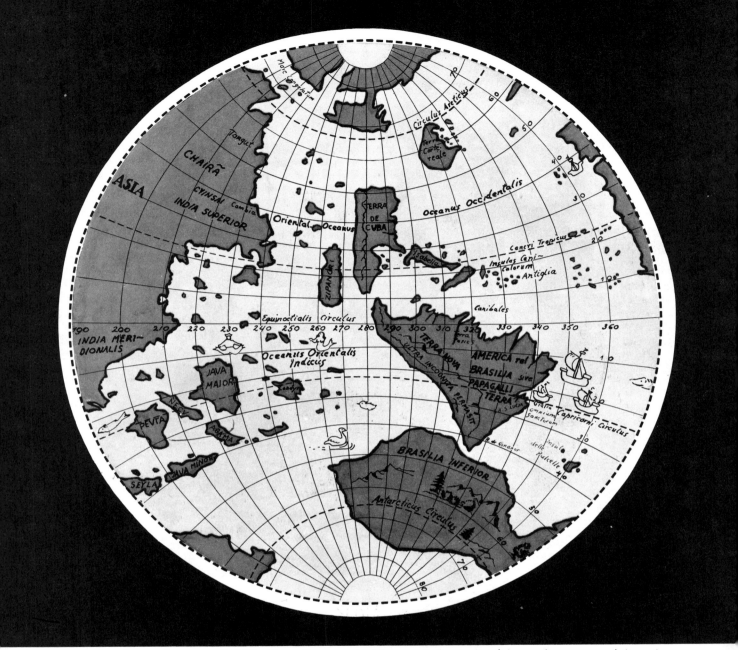

A map made about the year 1520. Magellan wanted to reach the Indies* by sailing around America.

the Atlantic Ocean to America. A Spaniard, Vasco Balboa,* saw a great sea when he was on America's western coast. I am sure that there is a passage that will lead me to this sea. I shall find this passage and sail westward until I reach the Spice Islands."

The King nodded thoughtfully. Then he asked, "What if you cannot find this passage?"

Magellan lifted his head proudly. "I have sailed on Portuguese ships around the southern tip of Africa to reach India," he said. "If I must, I shall sail around America in the same way. Nothing will stop me. I will bring honor to you and glory to Spain."

Rio de Janeiro, Brazil. This beautiful city lies along the bay where Magellan landed in 1519.

The courageous sea captain had convinced the King. Rising from his throne, the King said, "Ferdinand Magellan, you shall have ships, sailors, and supplies for your voyage westward to the Indies. May God go with you."

On a warm August morning in 1519, five ships sailed from Seville,* Spain. Standing on the deck of the flagship was Ferdinand Magellan. He guided his fleet across the vast Atlantic Ocean. On November 29, Magellan saw the coast of South America. (See map on page 51.)

For several weeks, the ships sailed down this rugged coast. Then they anchored in a beautiful bay, near the place where the city of Rio de Janeiro* is now located. There, the sailors went ashore to get food and water. Two weeks later, Magellan and his men continued southward. They explored many bays and rivers, searching for a passage to the western sea. By March it was cold and stormy, for soon the South American winter would begin. Magellan led his ships into a sheltered bay. He named it San Julián.* Here the Spaniards met people who were so large that they looked like giants. Magellan called these people Patagonians,* which means "big feet."

By this time, many of the men were tired and wanted to return to Spain. They complained that there was not enough food. Some of them planned to kill Magellan, but he discovered their plot. "We will sail southward," Magellan told his men, "even if we have to eat the leather of the ships' riggings!"

In October, Magellan reached a large bay. He sent two ships ahead to explore it. They returned with joyous news. They had found a deep, narrow passageway that led westward. This was the route to the western sea. Magellan led his fleet into the narrow winding channels of this rocky strait. The sailors on the largest

55

ship deserted their commander and sailed back to Spain. This left only three ships in Magellan's fleet, for one had been wrecked on the coast of South America. At last, after traveling more than 350 miles through the strait, Magellan saw the great western sea.

The small fleet sailed out of the strait into the calm waters of the vast ocean. Magellan named this ocean the Pacific, which means "peaceful." The ships sailed northward and then westward for more than three months. Only once in this time did the sailors find an island where they could get food and water. Even their drinking water was stale and yellow. Soon there was no more food, and the sailors searched anxiously for a place to land. They be-

The Strait of Magellan. Magellan found this waterway that connects the Atlantic and Pacific oceans.

Magellan led his small fleet through the Strait of Magellan into the Pacific Ocean.

came so hungry that they ate rats and sawdust. Finally, the starving men dragged the ships' riggings in the ocean. Then they cooked the water-softened leather and ate it greedily.

Magellan watched the horizon ahead and prayed that they would see land soon. By the time the ships reached a group of islands, most of the sailors were sick. Many had died. Magellan and his men remained at these islands for a few days to rest and gather food. Then they continued westward until they reached

Magellan reached the Philippine Islands on March 16, 1521.

the Philippines.* Most of the people here were friendly. However, one chieftain declared war. On April 27, 1521, Ferdinand Magellan was killed in a battle with some of the islanders.

After their leader's death, Magellan's men sailed on to the Spice Islands. (See map on page 51.) There they loaded their two remaining ships with valuable spices. One ship was wrecked

The Magellan Monument on Mactan Island in the Philippines, where Magellan was killed.

while trying to sail back to America. The other ship, the *Victoria*, sailed westward across the Indian Ocean. It was commanded by a seaman named Juan Sebastián del Cano. *

After sailing around the southern tip of Africa, the *Victoria* turned northward to Spain. It landed there on September 6, 1522 —about three years after leaving home. Of the 234 men who had started on the journey, only eighteen came back on the *Victoria*.

Although Magellan was not alive to see it, he had achieved his goal. He had found a westward route to the Indies. And his ship, the *Victoria*, was the first ever to sail around the world.

Juan Sebastián del Cano* sailed the "Victoria" back to Spain after Magellan's death.

Jacques Cartier hired fishermen from Saint-Malo* to help him search for a waterway to the Indies.*

CHAPTER EIGHT
JACQUES CARTIER
1491-1557

On a dark night in 1534, two ships were anchored near some small fishing boats in the harbor at Saint-Malo,* France. From the captain's cabin on one of the ships came the rumble of men's voices.

Lantern light flickered across the faces of several men who were seated around a large table in the center of the cabin. The men stopped talking and looked at each other uneasily, as the captain of the ship rose from his chair to speak. "Men," said Jacques Cartier quietly, "I am sure you know why I have asked you here. By now, many people in Saint-Malo know that the King of France has ordered me to sail west of Newfoundland to search for a sea route to the Indies.* He hopes that I will discover islands and countries where gold and other riches may be found. For this voyage, the King has given me money to hire two ships and a crew." Cartier paused for a moment, as he looked at each of the men before him. "I want you to sail with me on this voyage," he said. "Each of you will be well paid."

One of the men said quickly, "We are sailors and fishermen, not explorers!" The others nodded in agreement. "It is not that we do not trust you, Captain Cartier," the fisherman continued, "but this voyage is too dangerous. Each spring we sail to the fishing grounds near Newfoundland and come home with boatloads of fish. During these voyages, we have seen great icebergs near Newfoundland's eastern coast. Some explorers have sailed farther west into the foggy, ice-filled waters beyond Newfoundland and have never returned. We do not want to share their fate."

"Aye!" the rest of the men muttered. "We will not go."

Captain Cartier held up his hand to silence them. "There is one thing you men do not know," he said. "I have received another order from the King. This order will be read tomorrow before all of the people of Saint-Malo. It says that not one ship or fishing boat may leave this harbor until I have hired a crew."

"If we cannot fish, our families will starve!" said the men. Angrily, the fishermen talked together. Then, one by one, they rose and stood before the captain. "We have no choice," they said. "We shall sail with you, Captain Cartier."

The coast of Newfoundland. West of Newfoundland, Cartier hoped to find a sea route to the Indies.

It was a bright April morning in 1534 when Cartier's two ships sailed out of the harbor of Saint-Malo. Strong winds filled the sails and carried the ships westward across the Atlantic. Twenty days later, Jacques Cartier and his crew saw the coast of Newfoundland.

The explorers turned northward and entered the foggy strait that separates Newfoundland from the coast of Labrador. (See map on page 69.) Cartier guided the ships past huge icebergs that were drifting slowly through the strait. Finally, the explorers

Cartier landed in Canada in 1534. He set up a tall wooden cross and claimed the land for France.

reached a large body of water west of Newfoundland. This was the Gulf of Saint Lawrence, but to Cartier it looked like a sea. He turned southward along the western coast of Newfoundland before crossing the wide gulf. Then Cartier and his men sailed along the mainland of Canada for several weeks. In the ships' longboats* they explored each new bay, hoping to find a waterway to the Indies. In July, the explorers anchored their ships in a small bay and went ashore. There on the Gaspé Peninsula, Cartier set up a tall wooden cross and claimed the land for France. He named this region New France. Then the men returned to their ships and sailed northeastward through a dense fog.

Early in August, Cartier reached the northern coast of Anticosti Island. (See map on page 69.) Ahead of him he saw a great channel of water stretching far westward. "Is this the waterway that leads to the Indies?" Cartier wondered. He did not know that he had discovered the great Saint Lawrence River. Cartier longed to stay and explore it further, but he had found it too late. There was only enough food left for the long voyage home. Reluctantly, Cartier and his men began their homeward journey and reached Saint-Malo in September of 1534.

When the King of France heard about the great waterway Cartier had discovered, he, too, believed it might be a sea route to the Indies. He gave Cartier money to hire men and three ships to explore the waterway the following summer.

It was July of 1535 when Cartier once again sailed through the narrow strait between Newfoundland and Labrador, and entered the Gulf of Saint Lawrence. Aboard his ships were about a hundred men, and enough food and supplies for fifteen months. Soon the ships were sailing across the sparkling waters of the passage that Cartier hoped would lead him to the Indies. However, Cartier learned from two Indian fishermen that this was not a sea passage as he had thought, but a great river. Cartier and his men explored the mouth of the Saint Lawrence River for several days. Then they followed the river inland.

For nearly two months, the explorers sailed up the Saint Lawrence River, past fertile lands covered with tall trees. Where the river became narrower, Cartier anchored the two largest ships and left some of his men behind to build a strong fort for the winter. Then he continued up the Saint Lawrence in the smallest ship.

Friendly Indians led Cartier to their village near the foot of a high hill which he named Mount Royal.

Where the river became too shallow for this ship, Cartier and some of his men rowed farther upstream in small boats. Three days later, they reached a large island in the river. Here, more than a thousand Indians crowded along the shore to welcome them. The Indians believed that the Frenchmen were gods, for they had never seen white people before. They led the explorers to their village near the foot of a high hill.

After visiting this village for two days, Cartier and his men climbed to the top of the great hill. Cartier named this hill Mount Royal. Then the explorers traveled back down the Saint Lawrence to the fort the other men had built. The leaves were falling. Soon the river would be covered with ice.

The explorers lived at the fort all winter. Many of the men died from the cold and a terrible disease called scurvy.* By spring, most of their food and supplies were gone. Eagerly, the men waited for the ice on the river to melt. Then they began the long voyage back to France.

Montreal,* **Canada,** is built partly on the island in the Saint Lawrence that Cartier explored in 1535.

A farm along the Saint Lawrence. Many people from France settled on lands discovered by Cartier.

After his explorations in Canada, Jacques Cartier was convinced that the fertile lands of that country would make prosperous farms and villages for French colonists. In 1541, he sailed to Canada with five ships to start a colony on the Saint Lawrence River. There he built a strong fort and named it Bourg Royal. In the spring, he sailed back to France, believing that the colonists would be happy. However, the King of France had put a cruel man in charge of the colony. After a winter of terrible hardships and suffering, the

68

colonists that Cartier had left behind returned to France. Many years would pass before the French would have a permanent settlement in the New World.

Jacques Cartier did not find the gold and other riches of the Indies that he was seeking. His discovery was far more important. The great Saint Lawrence River that Cartier explored flows through fertile lands, rich in minerals and timber. These lands were held by France for many years. Today, this great region is part of Canada.

The explorations of Cartier gave France a claim to vast lands in North America.

LABRADOR

CANADA

ANTICOSTI I.

GASPÉ PENINSULA

GULF OF ST. LAWRENCE

NEWFOUNDLAND

1535

1534

1534

1536

Quebec

St. Lawrence R.

Montreal

NOVA SCOTIA

ATLANTIC

OCEAN

Hernando de Soto and his army of treasure seekers landed in Florida in May, 1539.

CHAPTER NINE
HERNANDO DE SOTO
1500?-1542

On May 25, 1539, nine Spanish ships anchored near Tampa Bay on the western coast of Florida. From the ships, over six hundred men looked eagerly at the inviting, green coast before them. The leaves of palm trees swayed gracefully in the gentle breeze. Magnolias and lilies grew everywhere. All seemed calm and peaceful, except for tall columns of black smoke that drifted toward the

The coast of Florida seemed calm and peaceful when De Soto's nine ships anchored near Tampa Bay.

sky. These were smoke signals made by Indians who lived along the Florida coast. The Indians were warning each other about the arrival of the Spanish ships.

A tall, handsome nobleman stood on the deck of one ship and studied the smoke signals. He was Hernando de Soto, the leader of the Spanish expedition. De Soto knew that some of the Indians who lived here might prove to be unfriendly. But he was not afraid. He and his men had left their homes in Spain, Portugal, and Cuba to search for gold in Florida. No one could stop them now. They would find their fortunes or die in the attempt.

De Soto's eyes blazed with excitement as he turned to his companions. "The Indians have seen us," he said, "but we have nothing to fear from them. They will not dare attack armed men on horseback. These people will be very useful to us. We can use them as guides, and as slaves to carry our baggage."

With a small group of men, De Soto went ashore. Then he ordered the men waiting on the ships to follow him. A great cheer rose from these men, for they were eager to begin searching for gold. They liked and trusted their bold, cheerful leader. He had returned from Peru several years before with rubies, gold, and silver. The men knew that De Soto hoped to find an even greater fortune in Florida. "Soon," they thought happily, "we will all be rich!"

Within a few days after they landed, these treasure hunters began their march through the green wilderness of Florida. In this army were noblemen, shopkeepers, and soldiers. All of them wore colorful uniforms. Some carried bright silken banners. Their shining armor sparkled in the sunlight. Many rode prancing horses. Here and there were Catholic priests wearing long robes. A herd of squealing pigs followed behind the army. If hunting should be poor, the pigs would be used as meat.

In the green wilderness of Florida, the treasure hunters hoped to find a great fortune in gold.

De Soto needed Indian guides who could help him find the gold he was seeking. But the Indians did not want to be slaves of the Spaniards. They fought bitterly when the Spaniards tried to capture members of their tribes. De Soto could not talk to these people. None of his men could speak their language.

One day, some of De Soto's men met a group of Indians wearing war paint and armed with bows and arrows. When the Spaniards attacked, all but one of the Indians ran away. "Wait!" this man cried in Spanish. "Do not kill me. I am a Christian!" Surprised, the men lowered their spears. He told them that his name was Juan Ortiz and that he was a Spaniard. Twelve years before, while exploring Florida, he had been captured by a cruel Indian chief. Later he had escaped, and a friendly Indian tribe had protected him. Eagerly, the Spaniards took Ortiz to De Soto.

73

The Tennessee River. De Soto's army marched through part of the region that is now Tennessee.

Now the explorers had someone with them who could talk to the Indians they met.

The Spaniards traveled from village to village, searching for gold. Most Indians they met were poor. The Spaniards often treated these people cruelly. They captured many of them to serve as slaves. If the Indians resisted, they were tortured or killed.

Hoping that De Soto would travel onward without harming them, some of the Indians spoke of rich gold mines to the north. De Soto led his men northeastward into the region we now call Georgia. Here they were greeted by Creek Indians, who wore cloth robes and lived in houses plastered with clay. These were the most prosperous Indians the Spaniards had seen. But they had no gold. Tired and homesick, De Soto's men trudged onward.

After crossing the wide Savannah River, De Soto reached a village ruled by a beautiful Indian princess. The princess gave the Spaniards food and invited them to stay in her village. She also gave them over three hundred pounds of pearls. In spite of this, De Soto was disappointed. There was still no gold. He forced the helpless princess to leave her village and go with his army. One night she and her servants escaped. With them they took a chest filled with the finest pearls.

De Soto and his men continued onward, determined to find gold. They marched through parts of what are now South Carolina, North Carolina, and Tennessee. (See map on page 76.) When they reached Alabama, they met a powerful Indian chief named Tuscaloosa. De Soto made Tuscaloosa a prisoner in his own

In Alabama many of De Soto's men were killed in a battle with Indians, but De Soto marched on.

village. The Indian chief pretended to be friendly toward the Spaniards. However, he was quietly waiting for a chance to regain his freedom.

One day, during an argument, a Spanish officer drew his sword and killed an Indian. Then Tuscaloosa's warriors attacked the Spaniards with clubs, and bows and arrows. The Spaniards fought desperately, and slowly drove the Indians back. Then they set fire to Tuscaloosa's village. The air was filled with the cries of men, women, and children being burned to death or trampled by frightened horses. At last, all of the Indians were dead. Eighty of De Soto's men had been killed also. Nearly all of the army's food and baggage, as well as the pearls from the princess, had been destroyed. Some of De Soto's frightened men wanted to go home. But De Soto paid no attention to their wishes. Within a month, his army marched again.

De Soto's explorations gave Spain a claim to much land in the southern part of North America.

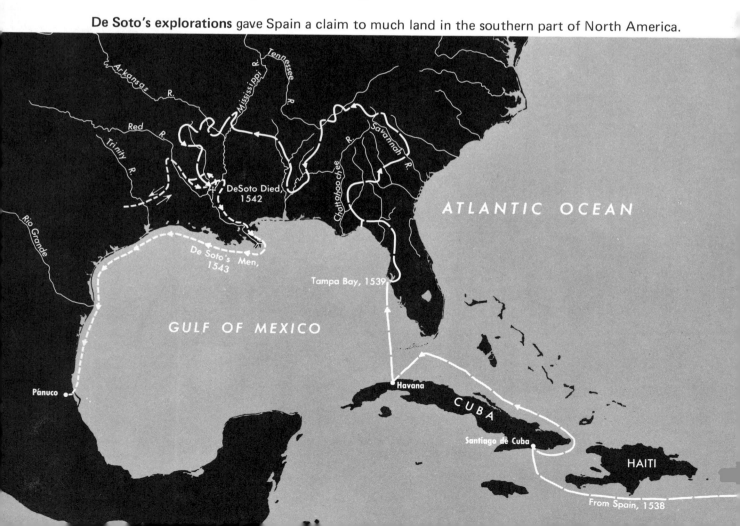

De Soto reached the Mississippi River in 1541, after two years of wandering.

On May 8, 1541—two years after they had begun their journey—the Spaniards reached the banks of a wide river. No Europeans had ever seen this waterway before. De Soto named it the Rio Grande, or "Great River." Today we call it the Mississippi. It is one of the longest rivers in the world.

The army crossed the Mississippi River and marched on into Arkansas. As the months passed, even De Soto became discouraged. Nearly half of his men had died, and many more were sick. There were only a few good horses left. Weary and disappointed, he led his men back to the Mississippi River. There, in the spring of 1542, Hernando de Soto died. His men buried him in the mighty river he had discovered.

Later, De Soto's men built crude boats and sailed down the Mississippi River. When they reached the Gulf of Mexico, they sailed along the coast for hundreds of miles. (See map on page 76.) In September of 1543, they finally reached a Spanish settlement. About three hundred sick and ragged men were all that remained of De Soto's proud army of treasure seekers.

The Mississippi River. After De Soto died in 1542, his men sailed down the Mississippi to the coast.

Henry Hudson's crew rebelled when he tried to sail his ship around northern Europe to reach China.

CHAPTER TEN
HENRY HUDSON
1575?-1611

Captain Henry Hudson could hear the angry voices of his crew. He turned to look at the men who had gathered on the deck of his small ship, the *Half Moon*. The sailors were huddled together, as if to shelter themselves from the icy winds that blew across the Arctic Ocean.

"I'll sail no farther north!" shouted one of the men. "Aye!" agreed the other sailors. Then, one of the men stepped forward. "Captain Hudson, we are freezing," he said. "Our hands and feet are numb from the cold. Some of us are afraid that the ship will be crushed by the ice. We want to go back to Holland before we lose our lives!"

"Men," said the tall, English sea captain, "I share the same hardships as you, but I am not afraid. I've sailed this northern ocean twice before, searching for a trade route to China. (See map on page 87.) This time, I hope that we shall be able to sail around northern Europe and reach Asia. The Dutch merchants who hired me are eager to find a northern route to the East* so that their ships can bring back the riches of those lands. Help me discover this route and you will receive much honor when we return to Holland."

"No!" the men shouted. "We'll freeze to death!"

Captain Hudson looked thoughtfully at his angry crew. He could see that they were determined to turn back. Then he thought of the maps of America he had in his cabin. For some time he had wanted to search for a western route to China along the coast of North America. "Perhaps," he thought, "this is my chance to find it."

"Men," said Captain Hudson, "I have a plan which may bring success to our voyage. We shall turn the ship around, but we shall not go back to Holland. Instead, let us search for a water route to China along the mainland of America. There are two choices. We can look for a way around the northernmost part of America, or we can search for a passage through America by sailing southward along its coast. You men may decide which route we shall take."

80

Icebergs and ice floes in the cold waters of the Arctic Ocean frightened Hudson's men.

"Let's go home, Captain!" cried one timid sailor.

A husky seaman tugged at the sailor's sleeve. "Quiet, you fool!" he whispered. "We shall be thrown into prison if we go home now. Men are sometimes hanged for refusing to follow their captain's orders."

The sailors argued among themselves for a time. Finally, one man called out, "We want to sail in warmer waters, Captain Hudson. We choose the southern route."

Henry Hudson made four voyages in search of a water route to China.

The tall Englishman smiled. Then he called his officers and ordered them to turn the ship around. "We are sailing to America," said Henry Hudson.

In July of 1609, the *Half Moon* reached the northeastern coast of North America. (See map on page 87.) Captain Hudson and his crew began sailing southward along the coast. They explored many bays and inlets, searching for a water passage to China. When they reached what is now North Carolina, they turned northward again. In September, they entered a deep, sheltered bay. Today, this bay is known as New York Harbor. New York, the largest city in the United States, lies along the harbor.

Manhattan Island from the air. Henry Hudson visited this island in 1609. Today it is part of the great city of New York. In the picture below, the Hudson River lies to the left of Manhattan Island. The East River lies to the right.

The Hudson River. The "Half Moon" sailed up this river as far as the present-day city of Albany.

At the northern end of the bay, Captain Hudson found a wide inlet. Perhaps this was the waterway he was seeking. Eagerly, he followed it inland. But as he did so, it grew narrower and the salt water became fresh. Hudson realized that this was not a sea passage across America, as he had hoped. Instead, it was a large river. Today we call it the Hudson River, in honor of this great explorer.

Captain Hudson wanted to see more of the beautiful, fertile country through which this river flowed. By late September, the *Half Moon* had sailed about 150 miles up the great river. Finally it reached the place where the city of Albany now stands. Here the river became too shallow for the ship to sail farther. Disappointed, the explorers traveled back down the river to the ocean.

With a brisk west wind filling the ship's sails, the *Half Moon* began the long voyage home.

Instead of returning to Holland, Henry Hudson landed at an English seaport. At once, he sent a report of his journey to his Dutch employers. He asked for money to make another voyage to America.

Meanwhile, the King of England had heard about Hudson's discoveries in North America. He would not allow Hudson to leave England. "This time your voyage shall be made for England, your own country," said the King. Eagerly, Hudson outfitted another ship and hired a crew. He did this with money that had been given to him by some English merchants. Hudson planned to continue his search for a northwest passage to China in the uncharted sea between Greenland and Labrador.

On April 17, 1610, Hudson's ship, the *Discovery*, left England. Among the people aboard were Henry Hudson's young son and some of the men who had sailed with Hudson to America before. Near the end of June, the explorers reached Hudson Strait. (See map on page 87.) In this wide channel, they saw great masses of floating ice. Some of Hudson's men were terrified. They wanted to sail back to England. But their brave captain was sure he had discovered a northwest passage to China at last. He guided the ship through the dangerous strait for about 450 miles. Then he entered a large body of water, which we now call Hudson Bay. Hudson sailed southward along its eastern shore to the southernmost end of the bay. For weeks he explored the swampy coastline. But he failed to find a waterway that would lead him farther west.

By this time, it was almost winter. Captain Hudson turned northward toward Hudson Strait, but he had waited too long. Freezing north winds blew across the bay, and ice began to form

A settlement along Hudson Strait. Hudson sailed through this strait and discovered Hudson Bay.

on the water. Hurriedly, the men found a little harbor and pulled the ship close to the shore for the winter. Days later, the ship was frozen fast in the ice.

That winter the explorers lived in a log hut they had built on the shore of the bay. By springtime, the men had little left to eat. Many of them were sick. In June, they sailed northward once again. However, some of the sailors were afraid that their captain did not intend to return home. They seized the ship. Then they put the brave explorer into a small boat with his son and seven loyal crew members and cast them adrift. Henry Hudson and his companions were never seen again.

Less than fifteeen years after Hudson's death, Dutch settlers came to America. They made their homes in the fertile lands that Hudson had claimed along the Hudson River. English sea captains later followed this great explorer's route to Hudson Bay. They returned home with shiploads of valuable furs. Henry Hudson had failed to find a new sea route to China. But his voyages brought wealth and new lands to Holland and England.

Hudson's voyages. Hudson Bay, Hudson Strait, and the Hudson River are named after Henry Hudson.

The Straits of Mackinac.* On the far shore of this channel was the Jesuit* mission of Saint Ignace.

CHAPTER ELEVEN
MARQUETTE AND JOLIET
1637-1675   1645-1700

A pine-scented breeze ruffled the waters of the channel that connects Lake Huron with Lake Michigan. In the dim light of early morning, pale spirals of smoke rose from a cluster of Indian lodges on the northern shore. Near the lodges was a log chapel. This small settlement was the Jesuit* mission of Saint Ignace.

89

Father Marquette came to Canada from France in 1666. He wanted to make the Indians become Christians. With Louis Joliet, he explored much of the Mississippi River.

A pageant at Saint Ignace. Here, Marquette and Joliet began their journey to find the Mississippi.

On this May morning in 1673, the settlement at Saint Ignace was crowded and noisy. Indian babies cried and clung to their mothers. Dogs barked. French fur traders, dressed in buckskins and soft moccasins, gathered in small groups and talked excitedly. Indian braves, wearing deerskins and necklaces of dyed porcupine quills, stood along a sandy beach. They watched curiously as five Frenchmen loaded supplies into two birch-bark canoes. The men carefully placed smoked meat and bags of dried corn into the frail canoes. Muskets* and packages of gunpowder and bullets were loaded next.

Nearby a slim young man, dressed in coarse gray clothing and a beaver hat, was kneeling on the beach. He was Louis Joliet, a French explorer. With expert fingers, Joliet tied strips of rawhide* tightly around a soft, leather pouch. The pouch held paper, pens, and charcoal for drawing maps and writing reports. Then he placed the pouch in one of the canoes and carefully covered it with animal skins to protect it from the water. At last, after putting a few bags of beads into the canoes, Joliet and his men were ready for the long journey that lay ahead.

A slender, young priest walked slowly toward the canoes. He was dressed in the long black robe of a Jesuit missionary. At the water's edge, he turned and looked back at the mission that had been his home. He had come here to tell the Indians about the Christian religion. Many of these people were now his friends. He raised his hand and blessed the men, women, and children who crowded along the shore. Then he turned and stepped into one of the canoes. This young priest was Father Jacques Marquette. He and Louis Joliet had been ordered by the Governor of New France to find and explore the great Mississippi River. During their journey, Father Marquette would visit the Indians and tell them about Christianity.

Swiftly the two canoes glided away from the shore. The men paused a moment to wave a last good-by. Then they began their long journey westward in search of the great Mississippi River.

For several days, Father Marquette and Joliet traveled along the northern shore of Lake Michigan. When they reached Green Bay, the explorers guided the canoes along the shore and entered the mouth of the Fox River. Day after day, the men paddled eagerly up this river. They knew they were nearing the village of the Mascouten* Indians. No white person had ever gone beyond

Friendly Mascouten* Indians led Father Marquette and Louis Joliet to the Wisconsin River.

this village. However, Father Marquette had heard that these Indians lived near a river called the Wisconsin. He and Joliet hoped that the Indians would show them this river, and that the Wisconsin River would lead them to the great Mississippi.

When Father Marquette and Joliet arrived at the Mascouten village, they were welcomed by the Indians. Then, two Indian braves led them up a stream and helped the explorers carry their canoes across a swampy plain to the Wisconsin River. For days, the explorers paddled down the slow-moving river. At last, the canoes swept past marshy banks and out into the swift current of a wide river. Joliet snatched off his hat and waved it joyfully in the air. "We have found it!" he shouted. "We have found the great Mississippi!" Father Marquette nodded, speechless with happiness, and looked eagerly about him. Here the great river was nearly a mile wide. Small islands, green with graceful willow trees, rose

The Wisconsin River. The explorers paddled down this river until they reached the Mississippi.

here and there above the river's muddy waters. In the distance were high, forested hills. Father Marquette murmured a little prayer of thanks. With God's help, he and Joliet would follow this great river to the sea.

Day after day, the small party of men paddled southward down the Mississippi. Father Marquette and Joliet stopped often and explored the land along the river. Joliet drew maps of the regions

The Mississippi River. Marquette and Joliet reached this great river on June 17, 1673.

had found and explored the great Mississippi River. Soon other explorers would follow their route into the great, unknown regions of the West. Later, settlers would come and build their homes in these lands.

Marquette lived in a log cabin near the Chicago River* during the winter of 1674-1675.

La Salle and the Governor of New France planned to build a great French empire in America.

CHAPTER TWELVE
RENÉ ROBERT CAVELIER, SIEUR DE LA SALLE
1643-1687

In the fortress at Quebec, Canada, a dark-haired man stood before
the Governor of the colony of New France. He was René Robert
Cavelier, Sieur de la Salle, a French explorer. "Your Excellency,"
he said, "I have just returned from France with good news. The
King has given me permission to travel to the mouth of the great
Mississippi River and claim the land through which it flows for

France." La Salle handed the Governor a document that was sealed with the King's emblem and dated May 12, 1678.

"I am happy that you were successful," said the Governor. "You have worked many years for this."

"That is true," La Salle agreed. "When I came to America twelve years ago, I was determined to earn money and to explore new

La Salle traded for furs. He was friendly to the Indians and learned to speak their language.

lands for France. At first I traded cloth, guns, and other goods for furs which the Indians brought me. I became their friend and learned to speak their language. Then I talked with the Indians about two great rivers to the south, the Ohio River and the great Mississippi. After traveling hundreds of miles, I reached the Ohio River. In sunny meadows near the Ohio, I saw great herds of buffalo grazing on the tall, rich grass. Deer and other game roamed the woods. The soil was rich. Here, French families could raise the same kind of crops they grow at home.

"Then I heard that Father Marquette and Louis Joliet had reached the Mississippi and had traveled far down that great river. They learned from the Indians that the Mississippi flows into the Gulf of Mexico."

La Salle paced restlessly about the room. "I shall follow the Mississippi all the way to the sea, Governor Frontenac!" he exclaimed. "When I reach the mouth of this river, I shall claim for France all the land through which it flows. Then the colony of New France will extend all the way to the Gulf of Mexico. I shall build forts wherever they are needed to protect this territory from the English and the Spanish. So that I can pay for building these forts, I will trade with the Indians for buffalo hides and furs in the new lands that I claim. French families can make their homes in this region. The great Mississippi River will become the highway by which our colonists may send products to Europe."

"That is a great plan, my friend," said the Governor. "I will help you all I can."

La Salle was eager to begin his journey to the mouth of the Mississippi. However, he first planned to build forts near the Great Lakes. From these forts his men could trade with the Indians for furs. He also planned to build a sailing ship. While he

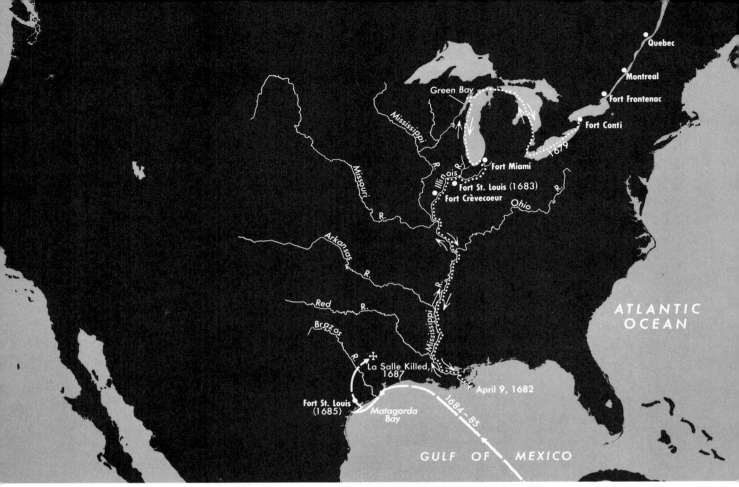

La Salle explored the Mississippi River all the way to the Gulf of Mexico.

traveled down the Mississippi, some of his men would take ship-loads of furs across the Great Lakes and sell them. With this money, La Salle would build forts along the Mississippi.

During that winter, La Salle's men built Fort Conti, near the southwestern end of Lake Ontario. (See map above.) They also built the *Griffin*, the first sailing ship on the Great Lakes.

In August of 1679, La Salle was ready to start his journey. He and his men sailed aboard the *Griffin* across Lake Erie and into Lake Huron. While crossing Lake Huron, the *Griffin* nearly sank during a fierce storm. At last, the travelers reached Green Bay on Lake Michigan. Here, La Salle's ship was loaded with furs that his men had obtained from the Indians. Then La Salle ordered the crew of the *Griffin* to take the furs back to Montreal.

La Salle built the "Griffin" to carry furs. It was the first sailing ship on the Great Lakes.

"Sell the furs," he told the crew. "We shall wait for you to bring supplies to us at the southern end of Lake Michigan. Then we will begin our journey to the Mississippi."

Near the southern end of Lake Michigan, La Salle and his men built Fort Miami. They waited there for weeks, but the *Griffin* did not come back. Finally, La Salle led his men southward. On the Illinois River, the explorers built Fort Crèvecoeur, which means "heartbreak." La Salle's men understood how much he had depended on the *Griffin* to bring the supplies they needed.

La Salle knew he must get supplies before he could begin his trip down the Mississippi. He chose five men and started on the long journey back to Montreal to discover what had happened to the *Griffin*.

The little party traveled for over two months through rain, sleet, and snow. After a trip of more than one thousand miles,

Lake Michigan. La Salle's ship, the "Griffin," disappeared during a trip on the Great Lakes.

La Salle reached Montreal. However, no one had heard of the *Griffin*. It was never seen again.

Even though La Salle had no money, he was still determined to complete the plans he had made. He borrowed money and bought the supplies he needed. Then he heard discouraging news. Most of the men he had left at Fort Crèvecoeur had deserted him. Only a few loyal members of his party remained. Hurriedly, La Salle began the long trip back to the fort.

When La Salle arrived at Fort Crèvecoeur, he found it in ruins. There was no sign of his faithful men. Finally, La Salle learned that they had gone north to Green Bay to escape from the warlike Iroquois Indians. La Salle traveled to Fort Miami. There, he helped friendly Indian tribes form an organization to protect themselves from the Iroquois.

In 1681, La Salle was ready for his trip to the mouth of the Mississippi. He chose twenty-three of his most trusted men and eighteen Indian warriors to go with him. They loaded supplies into large birch-bark canoes, and began their long journey. In February of 1682, they reached the Mississippi River. For over two months, the explorers paddled southward. Then La Salle and his men reached a place where the river branched off in three directions. Leaning over the side of his canoe, La Salle scooped up a handful of water and tasted it. The water was salty. They were close to the place where the river flows into the Gulf of Mexico. They had found the mouth of the Mississippi River.

La Salle told his men to land on the riverbank near a small hill. There they set up a tall, wooden post. On it La Salle carved the name of the King of France and the date, the ninth of April, 1682. His men buried a metal plate in the ground nearby. The plate was stamped with the royal emblem. Then they placed a wooden cross

La Salle set up a wooden post near the mouth of the Mississippi. He claimed the land for France.

beside it. In a clear, ringing voice La Salle said, "I claim this land in the name of King Louis XIV of France. I shall call this land Louisiana, in his honor." La Salle's dream had come true.

The explorers made the long return journey up the Mississippi and Illinois rivers. On a high cliff overlooking the Illinois, they built Fort Saint Louis. (See map on page 101.) La Salle was pleased. It seemed that all of his plans were succeeding.

However, La Salle was soon to be disappointed. His friend, the Governor of New France, had returned to Europe. He had been replaced by a man who was jealous of La Salle and who wanted him to fail. The new Governor ordered La Salle to return to

Starved Rock. La Salle built Fort Saint Louis on this cliff overlooking the Illinois River.

Quebec. He took away his forts and most of his property. The new Governor had convinced the King that La Salle could not help France. At once, La Salle sailed to France to appeal to the King in person.

When La Salle told the King what he had accomplished, the ruler was pleased with the daring explorer. He returned La Salle's forts and sent one of La Salle's men to take charge of them. He also approved of La Salle's plan to establish a colony at the mouth of the Mississippi River. The King gave La Salle four ships loaded with supplies for this colony.

In 1684, La Salle sailed back to America. With him were a hundred soldiers and the men, women, and children who would make their homes near the mouth of the Mississippi River. After La Salle and the colonists reached the Gulf of Mexico, however, they were unable to find the entrance to the river. In February of 1685, they landed on the shore of Matagorda Bay, Texas. (See map on page 101.) A few weeks later, some of the colonists sailed back to France. With one ship, La Salle and the others stayed behind to find the river.

The Mississippi at New Orleans. La Salle tried and failed to start a colony at the mouth of the Mississippi. Later, New Orleans was established on land he claimed for France.

La Salle landed on the coast of Texas after he failed to find the mouth of the Mississippi.

After they had built a fort near Matagorda Bay, La Salle and some of his men began the task of finding the Mississippi River. One group sailed along the coast, hoping to find the mouth of the river. However, the ship was wrecked in a storm.

La Salle led two different expeditions to the northeast, trying to find a stream that would flow into the Mississippi. If they could find the Mississippi, they would be able to travel up the river to the French settlements in Canada and get supplies. La Salle and his men walked hundreds of miles in search of the Mississippi, but they could not find it.

When La Salle returned from his last trip, he knew he must get help. Many of the colonists had died. Supplies were nearly gone. No ship had come from France to help them. In January of

1687, La Salle and about twenty men began a desperate journey to reach the fort he had built on the Illinois River. A few months later, La Salle was murdered by some of his own men.

La Salle's dream of a huge French colony in America did not come true, but he is still remembered as a great explorer. He claimed for his country the entire valley of the Mississippi. Soon after his death, France built the forts he had planned along this great river. For many years, France held the rich lands that had been claimed by René Robert Cavelier, Sieur de la Salle.

A statue of La Salle at Navasota, Texas. La Salle dreamed of establishing a great French colony in America. Although this dream did not come true, his explorations gave France a claim to vast territories in America.

Captain James Cook explored large areas of the Pacific Ocean during the eighteenth century.

CHAPTER THIRTEEN
CAPTAIN JAMES COOK
1728-1779

Captain James Cook entered the cabin of his small ship. In his hand were final instructions from the English navy for a voyage to the South Pacific Ocean. The navy had ordered him to sail the ship *Endeavour* past the southern tip of South America. Then he was to sail westward across the South Pacific to a newly discovered island called Tahiti. There, Captain Cook would assist the three scientists aboard his ship to observe a great scientific event.

Astronomers knew that on the third of June, 1769, the planet Venus would pass between the earth and the sun. By sending scientists to observe this event from different locations, they hoped to discover the sun's distance from the earth. The island of Tahiti was chosen as the place from which Captain Cook and the scientists aboard his ship would study the passage of Venus.

British scientists and the admirals of the Royal Navy had agreed that no one was better qualified to lead this expedition than James Cook. As a boy, he had taught himself mathematics, navigation, and astronomy. Later he made charts of the waters of the Saint Lawrence River. These had helped the English drive the French from the city of Quebec, Canada. A report that he had written about the moon's passage between the earth and the sun had been read before famous scientists in England. Cook also had many years' experience as a sailor, and he had commanded a ship in the Royal Navy. If anyone could safely lead an expedition to the other side of the world and back, it was James Cook.

Captain Cook walked to his desk and unlocked a small steel box. He took out a document that was sealed with wax and stamped with the emblem of the Royal Navy. No one but the admirals of the navy and Cook knew that he had received this second set of instructions. Captain Cook carefully broke the seal. As he read the message inside, he learned that he was to leave Tahiti as soon as the astronomers had watched Venus pass between the earth and the sun. He was to search for a great continent that geographers believed might be located in the South Pacific Ocean.

Captain Cook looked at his map of the South Pacific. From the map, he could see that most of this great ocean had never been explored by Europeans. A few irregular lines had been drawn to show the general location of the continent of Australia.

Captain Cook claimed the islands of New Zealand and the east coast of Australia for England.

New Zealand also had been discovered, but no one knew its size or shape.

"It is possible that there may be another continent in this ocean," Captain Cook thought. "The explorer who finds it will claim it for his country. This is why I have been given secret instructions. If there is such a land, England wants me to claim it."

James Cook began this great voyage in 1768. Nearly three years passed before he returned to England. During this time, he sailed all the way around the world. (See map on page 119.) He explored vast areas of the South Pacific Ocean between the continents of South America and Australia. Captain Cook did not find the "great southern continent" for which he was looking. However, he explored the entire coastline of New Zealand. Then he sailed along the eastern coast of Australia. Landing at an inlet called Botany Bay,* he claimed the land for England. Captain Cook drew maps showing the places he had visited. As a result of Cook's journey, England began sending colonists to Australia in the late 1780's.

Cook landed at Botany Bay, * in Australia. Later, he drew maps of Australia's eastern coast.

Antarctica.* Cook sailed farther south than any explorer before him, but he did not reach Antarctica.

In 1772, Captain Cook again sailed in search of the continent that geographers still believed was somewhere in the southernmost seas. This time, he sailed farther south than ever before. (See map on page 119.) In the cold waters of the Antarctic,* icebergs loomed up around his ship and icicles hung from its sails. Farther south, the sea was covered with thick ice. This was as far south as a ship could sail.

Captain Cook and his men sailed northward until the ship entered warmer waters. Then they turned eastward into the South Pacific. Though they discovered several islands, they still did not find the new continent for which they were searching. Finally, Captain Cook was convinced that if such a continent existed it must lie so near the South Pole that ships could not reach it.

When he was forty-eight years old, Captain James Cook began his third and last great voyage to the Pacific. On this voyage, he hoped to discover a water route called the "Northwest Passage," by which he could reach the Atlantic Ocean from the Pacific. Captain Cook believed he might find this passage somewhere in the arctic regions along the northern coast of North America.

From England, Captain Cook sailed around the southern tip of Africa, and then eastward past Australia into the Pacific Ocean. (See map on page 119.) Turning northward, Captain Cook explored

In the Arctic,* Captain Cook hoped to find a passage between the Pacific and the Atlantic oceans.

Cook landed in Hawaii. He believed these islands were his most important discovery in the Pacific.

the central areas of the Pacific on his way to North America. He and his crew became the first Europeans to visit the beautiful Hawaiian Islands.

Sunlight sparkled on the waves that washed the islands' shores. Palm leaves swayed in the gentle breeze. In the distance, Captain Cook saw beautiful, green mountains that were capped with snow. He was sure these islands were the most important discovery he had made in the Pacific. He longed to stay and explore them. Spring was coming soon, however, and he wanted to search for the Northwest Passage during the warmer months. Captain Cook

The Hawaiian Islands. Captain James Cook visited these islands in 1778, while he was on his way from New Zealand to the Arctic Ocean.

Cook explored Alaska's coast, searching for the Northwest Passage to the Atlantic Ocean. He sailed north until ice forced him to turn back.

left the Hawaiian Islands. In March of 1778, he reached America's northwestern coast.

For several months, Captain Cook sailed northward along the coast. (See map below.) He drew maps and named the capes and bays. Then he sailed through Bering Strait* into the icy waters of the Arctic Ocean. There he followed the northwestern coast of Alaska. The explorers sailed through thick, blinding fogs. Tons of floating ice drifted toward the ships. At last, a huge wall of ice blocked the way, and Captain Cook turned back. The short arctic summer was ending. He knew it was too dangerous to stay any longer in these cold, northern waters. He would continue his search for the Northwest Passage the following summer.

Cook's explorations and his maps gave the world a true picture of the geography of the Pacific.

Captain Cook left the arctic region and sailed back to the Hawaiian Islands. There, he and his crew became involved in a quarrel with some of the islanders. A fight broke out, and Cook was killed. The date of his death was February 14, 1779.

Today Captain Cook is remembered as one of England's greatest explorers. His three voyages added greatly to our knowledge of the Pacific Ocean and the polar regions of the world.

A monument to Captain Cook in Hawaii marks the place where this great explorer was killed.

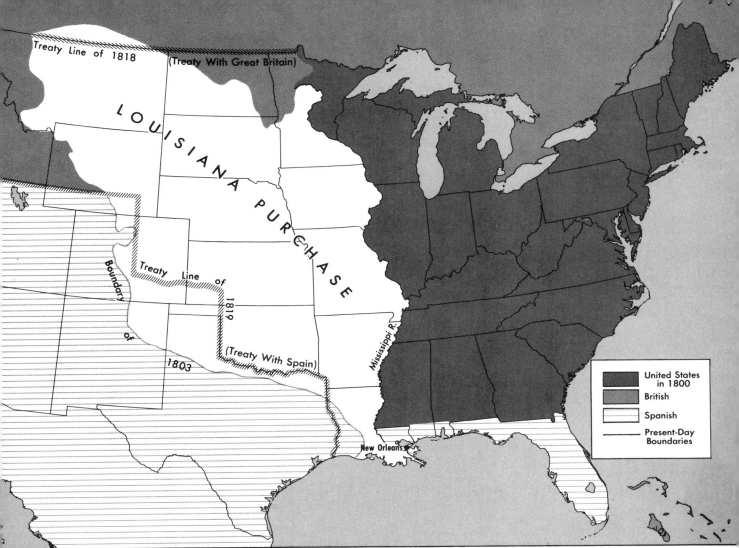

The Louisiana Purchase. In 1803, President Jefferson chose Lewis and Clark to explore this vast region.

CHAPTER FOURTEEN
LEWIS AND CLARK
1774-1809   1770-1838

Meriwether Lewis smiled as he entered the office of President Thomas Jefferson. "Mr. President," he said, "William Clark and I are almost ready to begin our journey to the Pacific Coast. We have medicine, rifles, and gifts for the Indians we may meet along the way. Men have been chosen to accompany us. Have you any final instructions?"

Thomas Jefferson pulled out a chair for his young visitor. "Be seated, Meriwether," he said. "You probably have already heard that France has sold the seaport of New Orleans and the whole Territory of Louisiana to the United States. (See map on page 121.) Now your expedition is even more important than we had believed.

"As you travel to the Pacific Coast, I want you to explore this great region which our nation has purchased. I want you to keep a diary in which you describe the Indians, the plants, the animals, and everything else you see. You can help the people of the United States learn about their new territory."

The Missouri joins the Mississippi near the place where Lewis and Clark began their journey in 1804.

Lewis collected plants along the shore as the three boats traveled up the Missouri.

In the fall of 1803, Meriwether Lewis and William Clark traveled to Saint Louis. Near the place where the Missouri River flows into the Mississippi, the men in the expedition built a camp. Here they lived throughout the winter. In May, 1804, Lewis and Clark began their long journey up the wide Missouri River with three boats and forty-three men.

The three boats moved slowly upstream against the swift current. Lewis often walked along the shore, collecting plants to send back to President Jefferson. Sometimes Clark joked with the crew. "Come on men, pull those oars," Clark would say. "We don't want anyone getting fat on this trip." The men worked hard, but travel upstream was slow and difficult. Often they had to get out of their boats and pull them over sand bars and fallen logs.

By October the river began to freeze, and the explorers had to look for a place to spend the winter. They built a fort near a settlement of friendly Mandan Indians, in the region we now call North Dakota. Here, two more people joined the expedition. One was a Canadian trapper named Toussaint Charbonneau,* who could

In a Mandan Indian lodge. Lewis and Clark spent the winter of 1804 near a Mandan Indian village.

A Plains Indian village. Lewis and Clark tried to make friends with all the Indians they met.

speak the language of the Indians. The other was his wife Sacagawea,* or "Bird Woman." Sacagawea was a Shoshone Indian who had been stolen from her tribe and sold to Charbonneau. Lewis and Clark knew that the Shoshones lived in the Rocky Mountains and could sell them horses. They hoped that Sacagawea could lead the expedition to the village of her people.

When spring came, the explorers continued up the Missouri River. As they traveled, Lewis drew maps of the regions through

125

which they passed. Many nights, when the others were sleeping, he and Clark sat by the fire and wrote in their diaries. They described buffalo, huge grizzly bears, and the fertile lands which they had seen. One day, Lewis climbed to the top of a high, rocky cliff along the riverbank. From there, he saw a jagged line of snow-covered peaks on the horizon. They were higher than any he had ever seen. These were the Rocky Mountains.

The explorers continued up the Missouri River toward the mountains until they came to a thundering waterfall. This was the Great Falls of the Missouri. Beyond it were more falls and

The Great Falls of the Missouri. The explorers carried their boats around these falls.

rapids. The men carried the boats overland until they reached calm waters. Then they paddled upstream for another month. Finally, they came to a place the Indians called Three Forks. Here, three rivers join to form the Missouri. (See map on page 132.) Lewis led the expedition up the western river, which he named the Jefferson.

Soon Sacagawea saw red, rocky cliffs which she had visited as a child. She knew her people must be nearby. Carrying her baby

In the Rockies. As Lewis and Clark continued westward, travel by boat became more difficult.

Friendly Indians gave the tired explorers horses and guided them across the Rocky Mountains.

boy on her back, she led the expedition farther and farther into the mountains. The river became so narrow and shallow that the boats scraped against the rocky river bed. Lewis and Clark looked anxiously for the Shoshones, for they needed horses now. Hunting was poor, and many days had passed since the men had eaten meat. They became so hungry and tired that it seemed they could not continue. Finally, Lewis and three of his men went ahead on foot. On the fourth day, they met a party of about sixty Indian horsemen. They were Shoshones.

Later, when Sacagawea saw the young Indian chief, she wept for joy and threw her arms around his neck. The chief was her brother. He agreed to help the expedition.

129

The Rocky Mountains. After many hardships, the explorers descended the western slopes of the Rockies.

With horses and a Shoshone guide, the explorers continued upward into the mountains. Day after day they climbed higher and higher. It seemed as though the trail would never end. Finally, the men stood on the top of a mountain and looked down at a winding river flowing westward. The explorers built canoes and paddled down the river. They were now west of the Louisiana Territory. At last, the explorers reached the wide Columbia River

130

and followed it to the Pacific Ocean. Lewis and Clark proudly raised the flag of the United States on the western coast of America.

A year and a half had passed since Lewis and Clark left Saint Louis, but they had completed only half of their journey. They spent the winter on the coast and in the spring started the long trip home. In the mountains they separated. One group, headed by Lewis, pushed northeast through the Rocky Mountains and explored a branch of the Missouri River. Clark and his men floated

The Columbia River. Lewis and Clark drifted down the wide Columbia River to the Pacific Ocean.

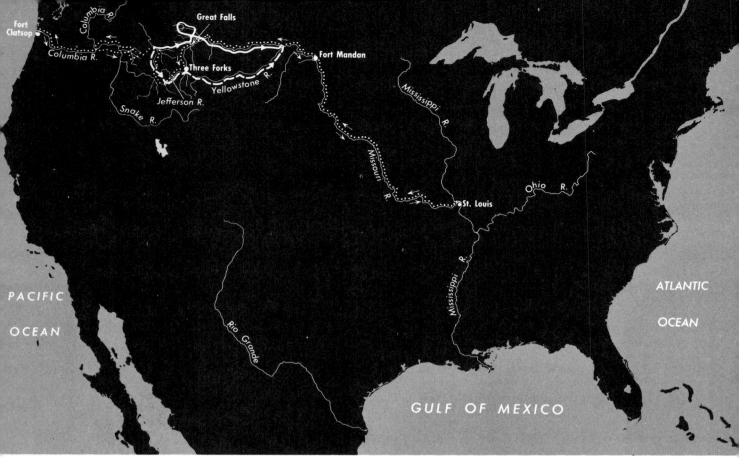

Lewis and Clark explored the Territory of Louisiana and the land west to the Pacific Coast.

down the Yellowstone River on rafts. The two groups met later, near the place where the Yellowstone flows into the Missouri River. When the explorers finally reached Saint Louis, on September 23, 1806, they had traveled nearly nine thousand miles.

Soon people all over the United States read in their newspapers about the thrilling adventures of Lewis and Clark. These two great men had explored much of the territory of Louisiana and had traveled on to the Pacific Ocean. Their accurate records and maps helped other explorers and settlers follow their trail into the West.

132

A monument to William Clark. The explorations of Lewis and Clark helped make the West a part of the United States.

WILLIAM CLARK

Robert E. Peary and his assistant, Matthew A. Henson. These brave American explorers and their four Eskimo companions were the first human beings ever to reach the North Pole.

CHAPTER FIFTEEN
PEARY AND HENSON
1856-1920　　　　　　　　　1867-1955

It was a cold, foggy afternoon in August of 1908. A small ship named the *Roosevelt* steamed northward from a harbor on the coast of Greenland. (See map on page 144.) A tall man with reddish hair and steel-gray eyes braced himself against the ship's rail. He drew his heavy coat tighter around his shoulders and sheltered his face from the salt spray. From his brisk manner it would be hard to tell he was fifty-two years old.

This man was the American explorer Robert E. Peary. He was planning to do something no one else had ever done. He was going to travel to the North Pole. Twice he had almost reached his goal. Twice he had been forced to turn back, saying to himself, "One more try!" This time he was determined to succeed.

Standing next to Peary was a handsome, rugged-looking black man. This was Matthew A. Henson, Peary's assistant. Henson, who was forty-two years old, had traveled with Peary on several other journeys to the arctic* regions. Peary knew that Henson's ancestors had come from tropical Africa. At first, he had

Peary's ship, the "Roosevelt," carried the American explorers as far as the Arctic Ocean.

wondered whether Henson would be able to stand the fierce cold of the Arctic. But Henson had quickly proved his worth. He was brave, hardworking, and always cheerful in the face of great dangers and hardships. Also, he was highly skilled at driving the dog teams that pulled the explorers' sleds over the arctic snows.

Peary and Henson were not the only people on this expedition, of course. Peary had brought five other American explorers, as well as a crew of twenty-two men to run the ship. There were also about forty Eskimo* men, women, and children who had boarded the ship in Greenland. Some of the Eskimo men would go with the explorers on the final stages of their journey to the Pole. Henson had the job of choosing the Eskimos who were to make the trip. Over the years, he had become greatly loved and respected by these people. He spoke the Eskimo language better than any of the other American explorers.

As Peary and Henson talked on deck, heavy fog swirled around the ship. It hid the sea from sight. Suddenly the people aboard felt a jarring crash. The ship had struck a large mass of floating ice. Slowly it broke through the ice and continued northward.

Peary nodded in satisfaction. He knew that his ship, the *Roosevelt*, could stand much heavier blows than this. After all, he had designed the ship himself. He had named it after the President of the United States, Theodore ("Teddy") Roosevelt—a man famed for his courage and determination. In some places, the sides of the ship were thirty inches thick. Iron and heavy timbers braced the hull. Part of the ship's bow was covered with steel, for it must break its way through about 350 miles of almost solid ice. This sturdy ship would take the explorers to the edge of the Arctic Ocean.

Robert E. Peary had made several journeys into the Arctic before he succeeded in reaching the North Pole.

Floating ice. The "Roosevelt" was built in such a way that ice could not easily damage it.

Mile after mile, the *Roosevelt* rammed and pushed through the thick ice that covers much of the sea between Greenland and Ellesmere Island. (See map on page 144.) "Rip 'em, Teddy! Bite 'em in two!" the ship's captain sometimes shouted as the sturdy little vessel fought its way northward.

In September, the explorers reached Cape Sheridan on the shore of the Arctic Ocean. "We'll see how much farther we can go," Peary thought to himself. Two miles beyond Cape Sheridan, the way was blocked by solid ice. This was as far north as the *Roosevelt* could safely travel. The explorers turned back to

At Cape Sheridan, the ice froze solid around the "Roosevelt." The explorers lived on board the ship for more than five months.

Cape Sheridan for the winter. Soon the ice that pressed tightly around the ship was frozen solid.

In October, the sun dipped below the horizon. The long arctic night had begun. During the winter days that followed, the explorers moved thousands of pounds of food and equipment to Cape Columbia, about ninety-three miles away. (See map on page 144.) They made igloos* with blocks of snow, to store the supplies they had brought from the ship. From this small camp, Peary planned to travel across the ice and snow to the North Pole.

Hauling supplies on dog sleds. Supplies were taken to Cape Columbia during the long winter.

Peary had made a careful plan for the long journey northward. He knew his plan must be perfect in every detail. One serious mistake would mean failure and perhaps death.

The North Pole lay in the middle of the Arctic Ocean, which was covered with ice the year around. The explorers and their dog teams must walk nearly five hundred miles over the jagged ice to reach the North Pole. Then they must make the long return journey. If they ran out of food or became too tired, they would fail. Before they left for the North Pole, every person understood Peary's plan thoroughly.

The people who left Cape Columbia would be divided into seven groups. Although they would all follow the same trail, each group would travel northward separately. The leading group would break a trail through the ice and snow. When these men became too tired to continue, another group would take the lead. Peary and the men in his group would always be last. He knew that they must save their energy for the final part of the dangerous journey. As they traveled northward, one group after another would be sent back to Cape Columbia. Peary and the others in his group would go on alone. By this time, there would be only enough food left for a few men to reach the North Pole.

About the end of January, the explorers saw a faint glow appear on the southern horizon. The arctic night was ending. In the following weeks the men loaded their sleds and traveled to Cape Columbia. They were ready to begin their long journey northward.

A freezing east wind was blowing across the Arctic Ocean as the explorers left Cape Columbia. Day after day they traveled northward over the frozen sea. Icy winds numbed their faces as they walked behind the heavily loaded sleds. At the end of each day's march, the weary explorers slept in igloos built by the men

The explorers traveled by dog sled nearly five hundred miles over the frozen Arctic Ocean.

in the leading groups. Weeks passed, and one group after another turned back to Cape Columbia.

At last, only two of the American explorers were left to make the final stage of the journey. These two were Peary and Henson. With them were four Eskimos, whose names were Ootah, Egingwah, Ooqueah, and Seegloo. They were still about 130 miles away from the North Pole.

Onward they struggled over the endless ridges of ice and snow. At ten o'clock on the morning of April 6, their goal was almost within reach. Only a few miles lay between them and the North Pole. This moment had been Peary's dream and goal for many years. Yet the past five weeks of constant travel and worry now

142

showed their effect on the fifty-two-year old explorer. He was too tired to go on. He had to stop and rest. After a few hours of sleep, Peary awoke and wrote in his diary: "The Pole at last . . . I cannot bring myself to realize it. It all seems so simple and commonplace."

That evening, Peary, Henson, and the Eskimos traveled the few more miles across the ice. Peary carefully checked his instruments and took several readings to determine his exact location. He and his companions had reached the North Pole. It was April 6, 1909, when the explorers proudly raised the Stars and Stripes of the United States at the top of the world.

The American flag flying at the North Pole. Matthew Henson is in the center of this picture. The other people are the four Eskimos who went all the way to the Pole with Peary and Henson.

The explorers spent thirty hours at the North Pole. Then they began the long trip southward. On April 23, they reached the camp at Cape Columbia. Peary wrote these words in his diary: "My life work is accomplished." The Americans Robert Peary and Matthew Henson had done what other explorers had been trying to do for nearly four hundred years.

The Peary-Henson expedition gave the world much scientific knowledge about the arctic region.

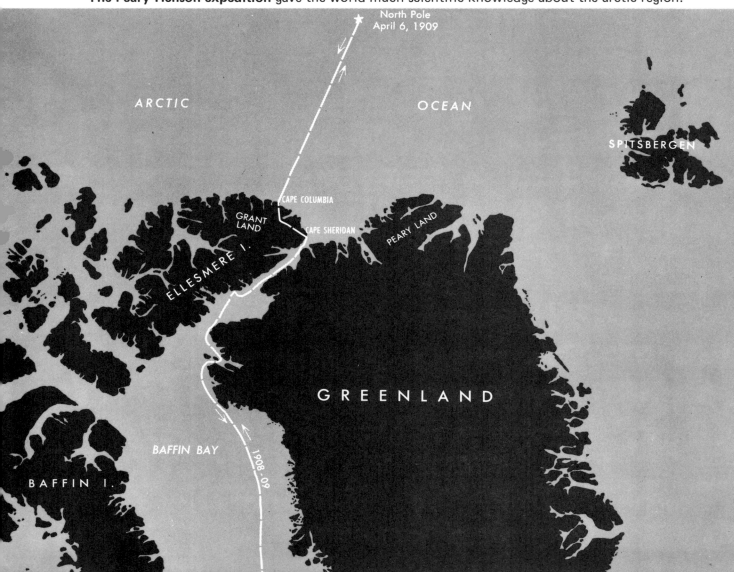

Neil Armstrong was the first person to step on the surface of the moon.

CHAPTER SIXTEEN
NEIL A. ARMSTRONG
1930-

What lies beyond our earth in the vast area we call space? Through the years, some people have made up stories in answer to this question. Others have looked up at the stars to see what answers they can give. In recent years, explorers called astronauts and cosmonauts have traveled into space to see what they can discover.

It has taken courage to explore space. To escape the earth's gravity,* astronauts must travel in spacecraft powered by flaming rockets. There is no air in space, and the temperature is freezing cold. Space travelers have to stay inside tightly-closed spacecraft that contain what is needed for life. If they leave their spacecraft, they must wear special protective clothing and carry a supply of oxygen* to breathe.

More than courage is needed to explore space. Spacecraft are guided by complicated instruments. The people who fly them need skill and training. They also need to be able to make wise decisions quickly in new and unknown situations.

Neil Armstrong, the first person to step on the moon, had these qualities. From the time he was a child, Neil wanted to fly. He took his first airplane ride when he was six years old. When he was nine, he began to build model airplanes. As a teenager in Wapakoneta, Ohio, he got a job after school to earn money for flying lessons. When he was sixteen, he passed his flying test and became a pilot.

After Neil graduated from high school in Wapakoneta, he entered Purdue University to study aeronautical* engineering. The Korean* War started about this time, and Neil Armstrong became a fighter pilot in the United States Navy. In three years, he flew nearly eighty combat flights in Korea. Once his jet was shot down behind enemy lines. Another time he flew a damaged plane to a safe landing on an aircraft carrier.

Neil Armstrong was a good pilot. He was so good that he was asked to become a test pilot after he left the Navy. As a test pilot, Neil flew many different kinds of airplanes. Most of them had never been flown before. It was his job to make sure they were safe to fly.

One of the airplanes Neil Armstrong flew was the X-15. This was a very special aircraft. It was part airplane and part rocket. In the X-15, Neil sometimes flew 4,000 miles an hour. He went as high as thirty-eight miles above the earth's surface. No other airplane had flown as fast or as high as the X-15. It was a dangerous job. A single mistake could mean instant death. But Neil Armstrong flew the X-15 without any accidents.

These experiences prepared Neil Armstrong for his next job — the job of exploring space. In the late 1950's, the United States had

Nine planets* circle the sun in space. In the late 1950's the United States and the Soviet Union began a race to see which country would be the leader in space exploration.

entered a race with the Soviet Union to see which country would be the leader in space exploration. The Soviets had begun this race by sending into space a round object with instruments that could send back information. This was Sputnik I, the first artificial satellite.* The United States had soon followed with a satellite named Explorer I. Soon both countries were launching spacecraft with people in them.

In 1966, Neil Armstrong was launched into space for the first time. His spacecraft was called Gemini 8. He and another astronaut, David Scott, were going to try something new. They were going to connect Gemini 8 with another spacecraft. During the test, however, something went wrong. Gemini 8 began to roll out of control.

A spacecraft is lifted into space by powerful rockets. It must move at a speed of 25,000 miles an hour in order to escape from the earth's gravity.* There is no air, food, or water in space. Travelers in space must take with them everything they need.

Quickly the astronauts changed course. They flew back to earth and landed safely in the ocean. Both men could have been killed in space. Neil Armstrong's quick thinking had saved them.

When space explorers returned to earth, their spacecraft splashed down in the ocean.

In 1969, Neil Armstrong began preparing for the greatest adventure of his life. He was to lead a mission to explore the moon in a spacecraft called Apollo 11. No one had ever been on the moon before. Many people believed it was impossible to go there. The moon is more than 240,000 miles from the earth. To get there, the astronauts had to depend on the work of thousands of people. Some built the spacecraft, and others tested it. Still others worked in the control center. Apollo 11 had more than a million parts. This meant that any one of a million things could go wrong.

Making a spacecraft. There are millions of complicated parts in a spacecraft.

Leaving for the moon. Astronauts wear special clothing to protect their bodies in space.

On July 16, 1969, Apollo 11 was launched at Cape Canaveral, Florida. Traveling with Neil Armstrong were two astronauts — Edwin Aldrin, Jr., and Michael Collins. Apollo 11 traveled at a speed of nearly 25,000 miles an hour. The trip to the moon took three days. By July 20, the astronauts were ready to land on the moon.

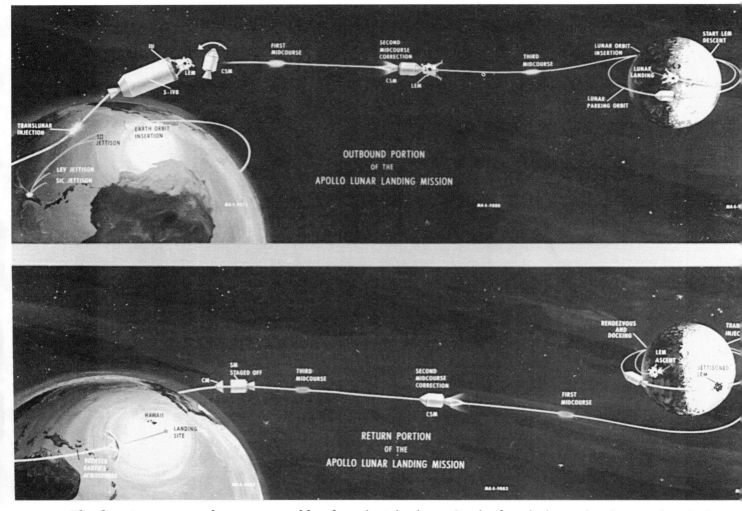

The first journey to the moon and back took eight days. On the fourth day, a landing craft called the *Eagle* separated from the spacecraft and landed on the surface of the moon.

Apollo 11 was made up of different sections. The astronauts' cabin was in a section called the command module. Attached to it was another section called a lunar module, which would separate from the spacecraft and land on the moon. This landing craft was named the *Eagle*. When the time came to prepare for landing, Neil Armstrong and Edwin Aldrin entered the *Eagle*. Michael Collins continued circling the moon in the command module. "The *Eagle* has wings!" radioed Armstrong as the two parts separated.

The *Eagle* moved toward the surface of the moon to land. But something was wrong. Neil saw that the area where the *Eagle* was supposed to land was covered with large rocks. If they tried to land there the *Eagle* would be damaged. There were only seconds left. The success of this voyage of exploration depended on him. With quick thinking Neil Armstrong took over the controls. He searched for a clear place to land. Skillfully he landed the *Eagle*. It settled gently on an area called the Sea of Tranquility, raising huge clouds of moon dust as it landed.

On the moon, the astronauts performed several experiments. In this picture, Edwin Aldrin, Jr., is setting up equipment to help scientists study a gas from the sun called solar wind.

The moon landing was being watched on television by millions of people on the earth. Neil Armstrong radioed back a simple message to these waiting listeners. "Tranquility Base here," he said. "The *Eagle* has landed."

After several hours of preparation, the door of the *Eagle* opened. Neil Armstrong climbed slowly down a ladder and set foot on the moon. As he stepped on its silent, unknown surface he said, "That's one small step for a man, one giant leap for mankind." It was a great moment. Like all the great explorers before him, Neil Armstrong had dared to go where no one had gone before. Soon other astronauts would follow to the new territories he explored.

The astronauts left this message for other explorers who would someday follow them to the moon.

HERE MEN FROM THE PLANET EARTH
FIRST SET FOOT UPON THE MOON
JULY 1969, A. D.
WE CAME IN PEACE FOR ALL MANKIND

NEIL A. ARMSTRONG
ASTRONAUT

MICHAEL COLLINS
ASTRONAUT

EDWIN E. ALDRIN, JR.
ASTRONAUT

RICHARD NIXON
PRESIDENT, UNITED STATES OF AMERICA

Why There Are No Chapters About Women

As you were reading this book, you probably noticed that there were no chapters about women. To understand why, you need to know about the position of women in the past. Throughout much of history, people in most places expected different things from women than they did from men. The role of a woman was generally to take care of the home and family. The role of a man was to go out to hunt or work or fight.

The position of women differed from place to place and from time to time. Generally, however, women had fewer rights than men. Women usually married very young. They received only the education they needed to do the kind of work expected of them. They were not encouraged to be adventuresome. In general, women in the past were expected to help men accomplish their goals. Their help was very important. In this book you learned about three explorers who would not have succeeded without the help of women. One was Columbus, who was helped by Queen Isabella of Spain. The others were Lewis and Clark, who were helped by an Indian woman named Sacagawea.

Today, the position of women in the United States and many other countries is changing. Girls now receive the same education as boys. They are no longer expected to remain at home after they grow up and marry. If you read a book about great explorers in the future, it will undoubtedly include chapters about women.

Great Explorers of the World

(Dates are years of explorations)

B.C. 2007 Hennu, an Egyptian explorer, sailed through the Red Sea to the Land of Punt, which was located somewhere on the coast of Somaliland in Africa.

? B.C.-A.D. 1200 Polynesians, brown-skinned people from Asia who discovered Hawaii and other islands in the Pacific Ocean.

A.D. 982? Eric the Red, a brave Viking chief, explored the southwestern coast of Greenland and founded the first Greenland settlement.

A.D. 1000? Leif Ericson. See Chapter 1.

1271-1295 Marco Polo. See Chapter 2.

1418-1460 Henry the Navigator. See Chapter 3.

1487-1488 Bartholomeu Dias, a Portuguese explorer, succeeded in sailing around the Cape of Good Hope at the southern tip of Africa.

1492-1504 Christopher Columbus. See Chapter 4.

1497 John Cabot. See Chapter 5.

1497-1507 Amerigo Vespucci of Italy supposedly made several voyages to North and South America. The new lands were named America in his honor.

1497-1498 Vasco da Gama. See Chapter 6.

1500-1501 Pedro Álvares Cabral of Portugal explored the coast of Brazil.

1513 Vasco Núñez de Balboa, a Spanish explorer, traveled across the Isthmus of Panama in Central America and reached the Pacific Ocean.

1513 Juan Ponce de León explored Florida's east and west coasts for Spain.

1519-1521 Hernando Cortes conquered Mexico for Spain.

1519-1521 Ferdinand Magellan. See Chapter 7.

1524 Giovanni da Verrazano, an Italian, explored the eastern coast of North America for France.

1526-1530 Sebastian Cabot, an Italian, explored South America's eastern coast.

1531-1535 Francisco Pizarro, a Spaniard, conquered Peru in South America.

1534-1536 Jacques Cartier. See Chapter 8.

1539-1542 Hernando de Soto. See Chapter 9.

1540-1542 Francisco Vásquez de Coronado of Spain explored a large area in what is now the southwestern part of the United States.

1541 Francisco de Orellana of Spain explored and named the Amazon River.

1576-1578 Martin Frobisher, an English explorer, searched the North American coast for a northwest passage to Asia.

1577-1580 Francis Drake sailed around the world for England.

1585-1587 John Davis (Davys), of England, explored the arctic regions of North America and sailed into Baffin Bay.

1596-1597 Willem Barents led a Dutch expedition to the Arctic Ocean and visited the islands of Spitsbergen.

1602-1607 Bartholomew Gosnold explored New England's coast in North America. He and Captain John Smith founded Jamestown, the first permanent English settlement in North America.

1603-1615 Samuel de Champlain, a Frenchman, explored Canada as far westward as Lake Huron. He also reached Lake Champlain and founded the city of Quebec, Canada.

1609-1611 Henry Hudson. See Chapter 10.

1615-1616 William Baffin, an Englishman, sailed far north along the northeastern coast of North America and explored Baffin Bay.

1642-1643 Abel Janszoon Tasman, a Dutch explorer, was the first European to visit Tasmania and New Zealand.

1673 Père Jacques Marquette and Louis Joliet. See Chapter 11.

1681-1682 René Robert Cavelier, Sieur de la Salle. See Chapter 12.

1728-1729 Vitus Bering of Denmark led a Russian expedition that explored the coast of northeastern Asia. He also sailed through the Bering Strait.

1731-1743 Pierre Gaultier de Varennes, Sieur de la Vérendrye, a French Canadian, explored a vast area in the central part of North America. Two of his sons may have been the first white people to see the Rocky Mountains.

1768-1770 James Bruce, a Scotsman, explored northeastern Africa and found one of the sources of the Nile River.

1768-1779 James Cook. See Chapter 13.

1789 Alexander Mackenzie, a Scotsman, explored northwestern Canada and traveled down the Mackenzie River.

1792 George Vancouver, an Englishman, sailed around Vancouver Island, near the Pacific Coast of North America.

1804-1806 Meriwether Lewis and William Clark. See Chapter 14.

1805-1807 Zebulon Montgomery Pike, an American, explored the upper Mississippi Valley and part of the Rocky Mountain region of the United States.

1842-1845 John Charles Frémont, an American, explored much of western North America. He became known as "the pathfinder."

1849-1873 David Livingstone, a Scotsman, explored much of central and southern Africa. He was the first European to see Victoria Falls, Lake Nyasa (Malawi), and the Zambezi River.

1858-1862 John McDouall Stuart, a Scottish explorer, made six trips into the interior of Australia.

1870-1885 Nikolai Przhevalski, a Russian, explored Mongolia and the western part of China, including Tibet.

1874-1877 Henry Morton Stanley, a Welshman, explored the region of the Congo (Zaire) River in central Africa.

1878-1879 Nils Nordenskjöld of Sweden was the first person to sail all the way along the Arctic Coast of Europe and Asia.

1888-1896 Fridtjof Nansen, a Norwegian explorer, was the first to cross the ice fields of Greenland. Later Nansen tried unsuccessfully to reach the North Pole.

1903-1926 Roald Amundsen, a Norwegian explorer who discovered the South Pole.

1907-1916 Ernest Henry Shackleton, an Irish explorer, led expeditions to Antarctica. He traveled to within 100 miles of the South Pole.

1908-1909 Robert Edwin Peary and Matthew Alexander Henson. See Chapter 15.

1911-1912 Robert Falcon Scott, an Englishman, reached the South Pole just 34 days after Roald Amundsen's expedition.

1913-1937 Donald Baxter MacMillan, an American, explored Greenland and the arctic regions of Canada.

1921-1930 Roy Chapman Andrews, an American, led several expeditions to the Gobi Desert and other regions in central Asia.

1926-1957 Richard Evelyn Byrd, an American, led several expeditions to Antarctica. He was the first person to fly over both the North and South poles.

1957-1958 Vivian Fuchs of Great Britain and **Edmund Hillary** of New Zealand were leaders of the first expedition to cross Antarctica by land. The trip took 99 days.

1961 Yuri A. Gagarin, a Russian cosmonaut, made the first flight into space.

1969 Neil A. Armstrong. See Chapter 16.

GLOSSARY

aeronautical (air uh NAW tih kuhl). Having to do with designing, making, or flying aircraft.

antarctic. Refers to the area around the South Pole. This area is called the Antarctic.

Antarctica. A continent that lies around the South Pole. (See **continent**.) Nearly all of it is covered with ice and snow.

Arab. Refers to a group of people who live mainly in northern Africa and southwestern Asia. These people speak a language called Arabic.

arctic. Refers to the area around the North Pole. This area is called the Arctic.

astrolabe (AS truh layb). An instrument used by sailors long ago to find their location when they were out of sight of land.

astronomy. The scientific study of stars, planets, and other objects in space.

Balboa (bal BO uh). **Vasco Núñez de,** 1475-1517. A Spanish explorer; the first European to see the eastern shore of the Pacific Ocean.

bazaar (buh ZAR). In Africa and Asia, a marketplace or a street lined with shops.

Bering Strait. A sea passage connecting the Pacific and Arctic oceans. It lies between Alaska and the northeastern tip of Asia.

bone needle. A needlelike tool made of bone. Used by Indian fishers to make and mend fishing nets.

Botany Bay. An inlet of the Pacific Ocean, on the southeastern coast of Australia.

cablegram. A message sent across the ocean by means of an underwater cable.

Cano (KAH noe), **Juan Sebastián del**. A Spanish sea captain.

Charbonneau (shar buhn NOE), **Toussaint.** A Canadian fur trapper who served as a guide for the Lewis and Clark expedition.

Chicago River. A small river in northeastern Illinois. The city of Chicago, Illinois, has grown up around this river.

circumference (ser KUM fer ens). The distance around something, such as a circle or a ball.

colony. A settlement outside the country that controls it.

compass. An instrument that people use to find the direction they are going. Many compasses have a needle that always points to the north.

compass rose. A small drawing put on a map to show directions. Here are three examples of compass roses:

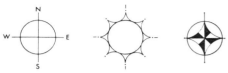

continent. One of the seven largest land areas on the earth. These are Europe, Asia, Africa, North America, South America, Australia, and Antarctica. Some people think of Europe and Asia as one continent, called Eurasia.

Dutch. People from Holland, a small country in northern Europe. Today Holland is called the Netherlands.

East. A name used by Europeans to refer to the countries of Asia, especially eastern Asia.

East Indies. A large group of islands lying off the southeastern coast of Asia, between the Indian Ocean and the Pacific Ocean.

equator (ee KWAY ter). An imaginary line around the earth, dividing it into a northern half and a southern half.

Eric the Red. A red-bearded Viking chief who started the first European settlement on the island of Greenland. See **Viking.**

Eskimo. Refers to a group of people who live in the far northern parts of North America and Asia. These people have light-brown skin, dark eyes, and straight, black hair.

expedition (eks puh DISH un). A group of explorers making a journey.

Genoa (JEN oh uh). A city in northern Italy.

gravity. The natural force that makes objects move toward the center of the earth. Gravity causes objects to have weight.

Great Lakes. Five huge lakes in the central part of North America. These are Lakes Superior, Michigan, Huron, Erie, and Ontario.

Great Wall of China. A huge wall, about 1,500 miles long, in northern China. It was built by the Chinese long ago to protect their lands from foreign invaders.

Haiti (HAY tee). The original Indian name for the island of Hispaniola in the West Indies. Today it refers to a country located on the western third of the island.

igloo. An Eskimo house (See **Eskimo.**) Some igloos are dome-shaped buildings made from blocks of hard snow.

Indies. A name used by early Europeans to refer to the lands of eastern and southern Asia.

Iroquois (EAR uh kwoi). A large group of Indians who once lived in eastern North America.

Islam (IS lum). One of the world's major religions. It was founded by an Arabian prophet named Mohammed, who was born in A.D. 570. Followers of Islam are called Moslems.

Jamaica (juh MAY kuh). A large island in the West Indies. See **West Indies.**

Jesuit (JEHZ yu it). Refers to the Society of Jesus, a religious organization of men within the Roman Catholic Church. Many early missionaries in North America were Jesuits.

Korean War, 1950-1953. A war between North Korea and South Korea, two countries in eastern Asia. The United Nations sent soldiers to help South Korea. Many of these soldiers were Americans. See **United Nations.**

Lisbon (LIZ bun). The capital and largest city of Portugal. It is a major seaport.

longboat. A large rowboat carried on a sailing ship.

Louisiana Purchase. A large territory that the United States bought from France in 1803.

Madeira (muh DEER uh) **Islands.** A group of islands in the Atlantic Ocean, about 600 miles southwest of Lisbon, Portugal.

Malindi (muh LIHN de). A seaport on the eastern coast of Africa.

Mandan (MAN dan). A tribe of Indians who once lived in what is now North Dakota.

Mascouten (mas KO ten). A tribe of Indians who once lived in Wisconsin, Illinois, and southern Michigan. Also known as the Potawatomi.

missionary (MISH uh nar ee). A person who is sent out by a religious group to persuade other people to follow the same religion.

Montreal (mahn tree AWL). The largest city in Canada. It lies on the Saint Lawrence River. The name Montreal comes from the French words for Mount Royal.

Moors. A group of people in northwestern Africa who follow the religion of Islam. They are a mixture of Arabs and other peoples. In the 700's, Spain was conquered by the Moors.

musket. A kind of gun used by soldiers and hunters before the rifle was developed.

Muslims (MUZ lihms). People who follow the religion of Islam. See **Islam.**

navigation (nav uh GA shun). The art of guiding a ship or an aircraft from one place to another.

New World. A name once used by Europeans to refer to North and South America.

nonfiction. Writing that deals with real people and events.

Norse. Refers to the people who lived in Scandinavia long ago. See **Scandinavia.**

Northwest Passage. A waterway around the northern end of North America, connecting the Atlantic Ocean with the Pacific Ocean.

Nova Scotia (NO vuh SKO shuh). One of Canada's provinces. Located on the Atlantic Coast.

observatory (ub ZER vuh tor ee). A building that has telescopes for studying the stars and other objects in space.

oxygen (AHK suh juhn). A colorless, odorless, tasteless gas. It makes up about one fifth of the air we breathe.

Palestine. A land on the east end of the Mediterranean Sea. The present-day country of Israel is now located in this area.

Patagonians (pat uh GO nih uhnz). People who live in Patagonia, a region near the southern tip of South America.

peninsula (puh NIN suh luh). An area of land that is almost surrounded by water. It is connected to a larger area of land.

Persia (PUHR zhuh). A country in southwestern Asia, today known as Iran.

Philippines (FIL uh peenz). A large group of islands in the Pacific Ocean, off the southeastern coast of Asia.

planet. Any one of the heavenly bodies that move around the sun. The nine main planets are Mercury, Venus, Earth, Mars, Jupiter, Saturn, Uranus, Neptune, and Pluto.

rawhide. Cattle skin that has not been tanned to make leather.

Rio de Janeiro (REE o day jhuh NAY row). A large seaport city in Brazil.

Sacagawea (sak uh guh WEE uh). A famous American Indian woman. She helped guide the Lewis and Clark expedition.

Sagres (SAH gresh). A village on the southwestern coast of Portugal.

Saint-Malo (suh MAHLOW). A seaport located along the coast of northwestern France.

San Julián (sahng hoo LYAHN). An inlet of the Atlantic Ocean, on the eastern coast of South America.

satellite. An object that revolves or travels around another object. An example is the moon, which travels around the earth.

Scandinavia (skan duh NAY vee uh). A large area in northern Europe that includes the countries of Norway, Sweden, and Denmark.

scurvy. A serious disease caused by the lack of fresh fruits and vegetables in a person's diet.

Seville (suh VIL). A port city on the Guadalquivir River in southwestern Spain.

Shangtu (SHAHNG DOO). A village in northeastern China. It was once the site of Emperor Kublai Khan's summer palace. The name of this village is now spelled Shangdu.

Shoshone (sho SHO nee). A tribe of Indians whose home is in the western part of the United States.

Spice Islands, or **Moluccas** (muh LUK uhz). A group of islands in the East Indies. See **East Indies.**

strait. A narrow waterway that connects two larger bodies of water.

Straits of Mackinac (MACK uh naw). A waterway that connects Lake Michigan with Lake Huron. See **Great Lakes.**

Tahiti (tuh HEE tee). An island in the South Pacific Ocean.

treaty. An agreement, usually in writing, between two or more nations.

United Nations. An organization of countries from all over the world. It was started in 1945 to work for world peace. About 160 countries now belong to the United Nations.

Venice (VEN is). A city in northern Italy.

Viking (VI king). Refers to people who lived along the seacoast in Scandinavia about one thousand years ago. See **Scandinavia.**

West Indies. A large group of islands in the Atlantic Ocean. They lie between the United States and South America.

Yangchow (YAHN JO). A city in eastern China. The name of this city is now spelled Yangzhou.

Index

Explanation of abbreviations used in this Index: *p* – picture   *m* – map